Paige G. Andrew, BA, MLS

Cataloging Sheet Maps
The Basics

Pre-publication
REVIEWS,
COMMENTARIES,
EVALUATIONS . . .

D0222831

"**A**ndrew brings to his new book, *Cataloging Sheet Maps*, not only his years of experience cataloging this special format, but also his background as a workshop instructor who has first-hand knowledge of the issues that present stumbling blocks to first-time map catalogers. After introducing maps and the benefits of cataloging them, he outlines the necessary tools and discusses the sources of information for the catalog record, contrasting them with those for cataloging monographs. He then proceeds through the fields of the record—fixed, coded, and variable—carefully explaining nontechnical phrases in the context of map cataloging and those more technical map concepts that are appropriate for detailed treatment at each stage along the way.

While the existing cataloging tools are comprehensive and helpful to the new map cataloger, they serve basically as reference sources—handbooks to check for answers to specific questions. The value of Andrew's work is its readable guidance and knowledgeable naviga- tion through the maze of AACR2R, *Cartographic Materials*, the *Map Cataloging Manual,* and MARC21. With his experience and familiarity, Andrew brings relative weight to the rules, applications, and instructions of the various official sources. He puts emphasis where needed and makes distinctions from the cataloging of monographs. He offers advice and comfort to the map cataloger by elaborating on the construction of geographic headings and headings with geographic qualifiers and subdivisions, and by referring to other relevant literature.

With the addition of a couple of specialty chapters and appendices with exercises in mathematical map data, geographical coding, and physical description, Andrew has made this an eminently useful source for new map catalogers to use on their own or as part of the curriculum in classes and workshops."

Nancy A. Kandoian, BA, MLS
Map Cataloger,
New York Public Library

"This book contains excellent guidance for the less-experienced map cataloger. Andrew takes what can seem to be a complex format and provides an easy-to-read explanation of the nuances of cataloging maps, giving the map cataloger confidence along the way. If dealing with scale and coordinates seems a daunting task, this book is the cataloging tool for you.

The excellent narrative reflects the author's enthusiasm for cataloging maps and imparts to the reader a wealth of knowledge. The extensive list of 'Tools of the Trade' and the tagging exercises are additional bonuses. Whether you are new to map cataloging or have new map catalogers on your staff, this book is a must-have."

Barbara Story, BA, MSLS
Cataloging Team Leader,
Geography and Map Division,
Library of Congress

"*Cataloging Sheet Maps: The Basics* is intended to introduce catalogers to the world of maps. It provides detailed guidelines on all aspects of map cataloging, including fixed-field coding, bibliographic description, authority control, and subject analysis. Additional chapters cover historical maps and special cases such as map series, supplementary items, and reproductions. The author covers every data element included in a full-level record and provides extensive examples (often with illustrations) of typical as well as exceptional cases. This thoroughness is the result of the author's familiarity with a wide variety of cartographic materials and his extensive experience in teaching map cataloging.

The author believes that cataloging requires the constant exercise of judgment by the cataloger. His text clearly illustrates how this works, by applying general rules and guidelines to exceptional cases. The readers of this book will gain not only a wealth of specific information about the rules for describing maps and how to apply them, but also a sense of the variety of cartographic resources and how to deal with unexpected situations."

John C. Attig, BA, MA, MALS
Authority Control Librarian,
Cataloging Services,
Pennsylvania State
University Libraries

"Andrew has provided an invaluable resource to those of us working in map collections. With fifteen years of map cataloging experience, he has truly emerged as the leader in this field. I found this book to be very informative and helpful. The author provides a step-by-step guide to the many elements of map cataloging and the numerous essential tools, both online and in print, needed for such. In addition, he includes the pertinent rules governing descriptive cataloging, useful rule interpretations, and many helpful examples of records and visual illustrations. Written with a basic level of cataloging knowledge assumed, *Cataloging Sheet Maps* will be an essential tool for those who are cataloging maps but have little or no formal training and/or technical support."

Susan M. Ewart Peschel, BA, MLS
Senior Academic Librarian
American Geographical Society Library,
University of Wisconsin–Milwaukee

The Haworth Information Press®
An Imprint of The Haworth Press
New York • London • Oxford

Cataloging Sheet Maps
The Basics

HAWORTH Cataloging & Classification
Ruth C. Carter, Senior Editor

Cataloging Sheet Maps
The Basics

Paige G. Andrew, BA, MLS

The Haworth Information Press®
An Imprint of The Haworth Press
New York • London • Oxford

Published by

The Haworth Information Press®, an imprint of The Haworth Press, Inc., 10 Alice Street, Binghamton, NY 13904-1580.

PUBLISHER'S NOTE
Due to the ever-changing nature of the Internet, Web site names and addresses, though verified to the best of the publisher's ability, should not be accepted as accurate without independent verification.

Cover design by Jennifer M. Gaska.

Library of Congress Cataloging-in-Publication Data

Andrew, Paige G.
    Cataloging sheet maps : the basics / Paige G. Andrew.
        p. cm.
    Includes bibliographical references and index.
    ISBN 0-7890-1482-3 (alk. paper)—ISBN 0-7890-1483-1 (pbk.)
    1. Cataloging of maps—Handbooks, manuals, etc. 2. MARC formats—Handbooks, manuals, etc. 3. Anglo-American cataloging rules—Handbooks, manuals, etc. 4. Classification—Maps—Handbooks, manuals, etc. I. Title.

Z695.6 .A55 2003
025.3'16—dc21

                                                                                                    2002068769

This book is dedicated to my sons, Ian and Colin,
and to my wife, Mary, who makes it possible,
with her patience, moral support, understanding,
and most of all love,
for me to succeed in my career
and the many activities that I pursue within it.

ABOUT THE AUTHOR

Paige G. Andrew, BA, MLS, is faculty Maps Cataloger at the Pennsylvania State University Libraries at University Park. Previously, he was Maps and Nonbook Materials Cataloger at the University of Georgia Libraries in Athens. Currently, Mr. Andrew is Chair of the Committee on Cataloging in the Special Libraries Association, Secretary of the Geography and Map Division, and a Director in the Central Pennsylvania Chapter of SLA. He is a Past Chair of SLA's Geography and Map Division and has served in various capacities for similar professional organizations, such as the North East Map Organization (NEMO) and the North American Cartographic Information Society (NACIS). He has published articles in *Cataloging & Classification Quarterly, Technical Services Quarterly, Catholic Library World,* and other respected professional journals, and has presented papers at ALA, SLA, NACIS, and other professional organizations. Mr. Andrew has also presented basic map cataloging workshops for the OCLC regional offices of PALINET, INCOLSA, BCR, and SOLINET and at institutions such as The Library of Virginia. Most recently, as Chair of the Library of Congress Program for Cooperative Cataloging's (PCC) Cartographic Materials Core Record Task Group, he guided a group of nationally known map catalogers in the creation of a new core-level bibliographic record standard for cartographic materials.

CONTENTS

Foreword

In this book, Mr. Andrew presents us with a user-friendly guide to the arcanery of map cataloging. Although we see maps everywhere in our environment, often we are unaware of their use or impact. Daily we see on the evening news or in the newspaper maps of weather patterns, recent political crisis areas, or earthquake epicenters. Subway, bus, and road maps are not unusual. But are we as clear with maps, as with books, about how they deliver information? Probably not, as cartography and geography have not been emphasized in public schools, colleges, and universities in the United States. Professionals in cartography have often had very purposefully to seek out work with maps, atlases, remote-sensing images, and geospatial data in libraries and elsewhere. Thus it is not unusual to find map collections in research libraries without map specialists as curators and, certainly, map catalogers.

Map librarianship is moving into a new world of computer and digital mapping. "Legacy" or paper map collections are less and less seen as valuable stand-alone collections worthy of a specialist curator. Map collections are now often housed with government document or social science collections, sometimes without benefit of a cartographically oriented staff.

This book, although helpful to the old hand as a "ready reference" tool, is most useful to library staff who commonly deal only peripherally with maps, and who need and would welcome Mr. Andrew's practical advice on the cataloging of cartographic materials. Those new to cataloging hard-copy maps, such as government document, social science and history catalogers, who are now asked to handle cartographic materials will find this book to be the very guide they need to approach describing sheet maps comfortably.

Because maps are graphic tools and receive their value in their graphic presentation of information, they cannot be cataloged simply using the cataloging rules for books. The differences are fewer than we might imagine, but they are critical in nature. For instance, with maps we must be aware of their number, size, and scale to sort out how much detail is available even before we see them. If these elements are noted correctly in the cataloging process, we can gauge the utility of the map for our purposes and decide whether to pull it from the collection for our use. Also, as more bibliographic records for maps are added to our online catalogs, it is equally important to provide accurate title access when more than one title exists, as well as proper subject terms to bring those maps of the same geographic and/or topical nature together for accurate retrieval by our patrons.

Complementing a shelf load of earlier publications, cited in Mr. Andrew's bibliography, this book synthesizes for the cataloger of cartographic materials many streams of cataloging knowledge and, along with his many teaching and workshop experiences, pulls them together into one coherent, useful, practical manual. Literally a how-to guide at the field level of the bibliographic record, this book is the first of its kind for map cataloging.

With globalization and instant communications around the world we are aware, more and more, of the efficiency of the cartographic image to display information. Cataloging these materials to make them accessible to the widest possible audience surely will enable us all to make wiser use of natural and human resources, both locally and globally.

Bon voyage!

Alice C. Hudson
Chief, Map Division
The New York Public Library

Preface

Part of being a professional is imparting one's knowledge and experience to those who are "coming on board" in the profession, in this case, as map catalogers. I am pleased to fulfill one of my professional responsibilities through the writing of this book, for it allows me to impart fifteen years of map cataloging experience to those who are new to, or inexperienced with, working with sheet maps. I have had the privilege over the past few years to teach basic map cataloging workshops throughout the country. This book is a natural extension of the process of teaching others in a personal setting.

The primary goal of the book is to provide the reader with step-by-step guidelines in applying cataloging rules and rule interpretations, while creating full-level and accurate bibliographic descriptions for sheet maps. A secondary, though nonetheless important, goal is to provide a sense of confidence in working with maps by dispelling some of the misconceptions regarding their level of complexity. You will find that cataloging maps, in terms of the number of unique fields involved, is not far removed from cataloging a monograph.

This book was written with some assumptions about the reader in mind. Those assumptions include some level of cataloging experience with another format of material, likely monographs; knowledge of and experience with MARC 21 and the ability to apply information to a variety of fixed and variable fields; experience in using and creating records for OCLC; and possession of copies of the basic tools necessary for cataloging, such as the *Anglo-American Cataloguing Rules,* Second Edition, Revised, and the *Library of Congress Rule Interpretations,* among others. At the same time, it is supposed that the reader has, although this certainly is not a requirement, access to the Internet, where many more of our tools and related resources are located.

Allow me at this point to share with you what this book will *not* cover, so that there is less possible confusion, although the gained experience in cataloging maps will transfer to other similar materials. Serially issued maps, atlases, globes, and digital cartographic materials fall outside the scope of this book. Map series are covered on a very limited basis where necessary, particularly in regard to their physical description and mathematical data, but specifics relating to series headings and their application are not covered.

In addition, you will find that this book includes a necessary dose of "cataloger's judgment," for I believe in being flexible within the bounds of the rules that we use, as well as in applying common sense where needed. This is by no means to say that the tenets of the *Anglo-American Cataloguing Rules* or the application of OCLC standards and/or other standards are to be ignored or flaunted but, instead, reflects the reality that no book, including this one, can possibly cover every type of situation and nuance that the cataloger finds in working with maps. These nuances are due in large part to the fact that maps are primarily graphic in nature, rather than textual, and, in reality, their physical sizes are nonstandard, whereas monographs tend to be produced more often within a standard set of sizes.

Let me assure you that as you learn to catalog sheet maps, you are not alone in pursuit of this new knowledge and experience. Not only is there a cartographic librarian's online listserver open to all who have map cataloging questions, but individuals such as myself are always happy to answer individual queries as well. The MAPS-L listserver can be joined by sending a subscribe message to <MAPS-L@LISTSERV.UGA.EDU> using the standard form of text in the message area of "subscribe MAPS-L [first name] [last name]". Another avenue for reaching individual experienced map catalogers is to contact the president of one of several national or regional map librarians organizations; he or she can then put you in touch with someone or point you to an online "toolbox" that contains e-mail and other contact information, e.g., the "Map Librarian's Toolbox" that is part of the Western Association of Map Libraries' online Web site. Also, keep in mind that those map catalogers who are experienced started as you have, with no experience and much anxiety.

Finally, an open and inquiring attitude toward working with maps will take you one large step toward achieving this new set of cataloging skills. Naturally, the more types of maps and numbers of maps that you work with, the more comfortable the process becomes. I am positive that you will find the nature of maps to be always interesting and intriguing, and creating descriptions for them to be challenging, but never dull.

Acknowledgments

I would like to acknowledge the contributions of a number of individuals who in many ways, large and small, made the outcome of this book more accurate and precise. Without their assistance the final product likely would have been lacking in accuracy and/or content. John Attig; John Hamilton; Richard Fox; my colleague, compatriot, and fellow "weird cataloger" Rob Freeborn; Kay G. Johnson; Nancy Kandoian; Mary Lynette Larsgaard; Shirley Loo; Dorothy McGarry; Susan Moore; Rebecca Mugridge; Linda Musser, earth and mineral sciences librarian extraordinaire; Susan Peschel; Celia Pratt; Barbara Story; Chris Thiry; and Kathy Weimer. Thanks also to my map cataloging teammates, John Hamilton, Charlene Hitchcock, Susan Houser, and Colleen Smith, who have always supported my research and writing and other faculty efforts, even when we are sometimes overwhelmed with cataloging projects and daily work.

Special thanks go to my mentors (and friends) in map cataloging, Mary Larsgaard, Elizabeth (Betsy) Mangan, and Barbara Story, who taught me, opened doors for me, provided insights, answered questions, and simply are there to understand the everyday stresses and quirks of map cataloging.

Thanks also go to those who gave me a start in cataloging maps and have given me a hand along the way as I became more experienced: my first supervisor and friend to this day, Josephine Davidson; Arlyn Booth; Ellen Caplan; HelenJane Armstrong; Nancy Kandoian; and Alice Hudson.

Finally, I must acknowledge with great appreciation the colleagues, supervisors, and administrators at my institution and "second home," the Pennsylvania State University Libraries, for allowing me time and encouraging me to write this book. Some of these individuals are Judy Hewes, Rebecca Mugridge, Rosann Bazirjian, Sally Kalin, Dean Nancy Eaton, and, most especially, Marie Bednar.

SECTION I:
IN THE BEGINNING

Chapter 1

Background

Over the past two decades a trend has emerged in libraries, and that trend has been fast-forwarded due in large part to the computer revolution in our information age. The ability to collect, manipulate, and share vast quantities of data electronically has assisted most libraries with one bothersome area of responsibility—catching up with backlogs of materials waiting to be cataloged. The first materials to be addressed at the start of this trend, eliminating library backlogs through retrospective as well as current cataloging activities, most usually were monographs. After several years research libraries managed to eliminate their monograph backlogs, and then they turned to other materials, usually "nonbook" formats such as audiovisual items and music.

Maps and other cartographic materials typically have come last on the list of backlogged materials waiting to be cataloged. It is only within the past decade that several large research libraries with significant map collections tackled and completed cataloging and/or retrospective conversions of sheet maps. Collections at institutions such as the University of Washington, the University of Georgia, and the Colorado School of Mines, among others, are completely cataloged and available online, while many other institutions, such as Ball State University and The Pennsylvania State University, are currently attempting to complete their map collection backlogs.

Consequently, as the value of sheet maps continues to grow, and more library administrators become aware of their value and the variety of information to be found in their content, more individuals need training to do the cataloging and classification work necessary to place bibliographic records for maps in online catalogs, making them infinitely more accessible. One sure sign that the trend of eliminating backlogs has finally caught up to sheet maps and other cartographic materials is the growing number and increasing regularity of workshops offered by many Online Computer Library Center (OCLC) regional network offices. I've been fortunate to be an instructor for a number of basic map cataloging workshops in the past five years, and it is gratifying to know that now many more individuals are working hard to make sheet maps available to the broader world through their newfound map cataloging skills.

This book is intended primarily to assist catalogers with little or no experience in creating descriptive bibliographic records for sheet maps. It is also intended to assist those map librarians with cataloging responsibilities who only occasionally find time to catalog maps and need a ready reference source. It is expected that the user/reader of this text already has knowledge of, and experience using, the machine-readable cataloging (MARC) format and catalogs on the international bibliographic utility, OCLC. However, if you catalog at the local level or on another bibliographic utility, you still will find this book useful for your purposes.

Why don't we start at the beginning? That is to say, what is it about a map, as an item that imparts its information to the user in a graphic, rather than textual, form, that makes it either unique opposed to other forms of information or seemingly difficult to describe accurately? To put it even more succinctly, just what is a map? Also, and just as important, why should we take the time to catalog something which contains both scientific and artistic elements and which usually comes in a cumbersome "package"?

WHAT IS A MAP?

The answers given here to the earlier question "What is a map?" not only provide us a working definition but also shed light on why we must understand some of the technical aspects of a map before we can accurately describe one. Understanding such things as scale and coordinates has a direct bearing not only on why they must be included in a bibliographic description but also on learning how to format and code this type of information correctly in both the variable and fixed fields. We necessarily have to pay close attention to titles and variations of titles, who is responsible for the creation of the maps, and describing the maps' physical properties because these are the areas that make them unique from monographs and other information formats. In addition, the G-Schedule, as you will see, is a different type of classification system within the overall Library of Congress classification scheme, as opposed to most of the other schedules, and rightly so. You will find that with time and experience in dealing with the special properties of maps makes this format of material easier to work with as well as fun and interesting.

The following quotes from three different sources will help you further understand the unique properties of maps, especially in relation to projection and scale. Reasons as to why maps are an extremely important form of information are also provided.

> The word "map" is derived from the Latin mappa, signifying a "napkin or cloth (on which maps were painted)." In turn, the term mappa can be traced back to ancient Carthage where it meant "signal cloth." ... Why is the map an abbreviated abstraction of the real earth? In order to function as an effective communication tool, the map must represent a large unit of the earth's surface upon a manageable sheet of material, usually paper. In transferring information from the earth to the map, an attempt is made to preserve four important properties: (1) true distance, (2) true shape, (3) true area, and (4) true direction. One of the problems the cartographer faces is that no singular map projection can possess all four of these properties at the same time. Therefore, the map projection and the map scale chosen should be the ones that best preserve reality while, at the same time, they suit the purpose for which the map was designed. (Drazniowsky, 1975, pp. 88-89)

> What is it about a map, that beautiful, awkward, supremely useful graphic form, that inspires us to become map librarians? A map is an attempt at the impossible, for it tries to depict a three-dimensional, curved surface on a two-dimensional flat surface. ... Perhaps another part of this is that both a map and a painting are in the first place a flat sheet of medium, which yet both take advantage of our thinking in pictures; neither one can reproduce exactly the infinite variety and complexity of reality, they *must* speak in metaphor, with the worker selecting the part of reality he chooses to depict, sacrificing some measure of truth in one dimension to show it faithfully in another . . . and all this at a much reduced scale, particularly in maps. (Larsgaard, 1978, p. 227)

The rapidly growing population of the earth and the increasing complexity of modern life, with its attendant pressures and contentions for available resources, has made necessary detailed studies of the physical and social environment. . . . The geographer, preeminently, as well as the planner, historian, economist, agriculturalist, geologist, and others working in the basic sciences and engineering, long ago found the map to be an indispensable aid.

. . . A large map of a small region, depicting its land forms, drainage, vegetation, settlement patterns, roads, geology, or a host of other detailed distributions, makes available the knowledge of the relationships necessary to plan and carry on many works intelligently.

. . . Whatever the kind of map, cartography can be succinctly described as the art, science, and technology of making maps of the earth or other celestial bodies. . . . [A] map is a unique form of communication; cartography has developed a distinct body of theory and practice that includes a series of processes that are peculiarly cartographic and common to the making of all maps.

. . . All maps are reductions. This means that the first decision of the cartographer must have to do with the dimensional relationship between reality and the map; this is called "scale." . . . By their very nature all maps are the presentation of spatial relationships. Therefore, another of the cartographer's distinctive tasks is to employ a transformation of the spherical surface that changes it into a plane. . . . A system of transformation from the spherical to the plane surface is called a map projection. (Robinson, Sale, and Morrison, 1978, pp. 4-5)

WHY BOTHER TO CATALOG SHEET MAPS?

The obvious short answer to this question is because the library has taken the time, effort, and expense to collect this type of information, and, therefore, it should be made available to the library's patrons, as is any other kind of library material. Of course, cataloging any material is a costly process, so when an administrator asks this question, dollar signs are usually on his or her mind, and strong justifications typically need to be offered.

One of these justifications involves the increase in use of Geographic Information Systems (GIS). As Andrew and Hall (1999) state:

Perhaps this can in part be attributed to the proliferation of Geographic Information Systems ... and other digital forms of cartographic information such as electronic atlases, which tends to raise awareness as to the extreme value and existence of location-based information, including maps and atlases. Maps, as a visual representation of the Earth's or other celestial body's surface or subsurface, provide an additional method of presenting information for research and other needs. It has been noted that at least 80 percent of all information contains a direct link to "place," making cartographic material that much more important to our users. (p. 13)

Of course, other reasons are available to answer this question. For example, it is always valuable to know what is in a given collection, and cataloging provides an "inventory" for this use. This allows also for a more accurate collection development scheme because facilitating online retrieval can show the map librarian the relative strengths and weaknesses of the collection. In addition, as personnel leave a library, their knowledge of the collection, how it was begun, policies and procedures that were created and changed, and the goals for its future can be lost. Therefore, a cataloged map collection, as with any collection, is available to help reconstruct or at least maintain the life of the collection until the next collection manager is in place.

Finally, our current paper maps do, and will continue to, serve as the original repository of information for future electronic forms of cartographic information.

Besides the practical values of cataloging the map collection, libraries have come to understand that without maps as primary material much of the data contained within them could not be mined for the purposes of creating the digital data and mapping capabilities we have come to expect and use. From these combined desires outlined above comes the need to provide bibliographic control for maps and atlases, for without the creation of bibliographic records the ability to identify and locate needed items in the map collection becomes an overwhelming task. (Andrew and Hall, 1999, p. 13)

Chapter 2

Introduction to Map Cataloging

Speaking from a very biased point of view, what a joy to catalog maps! To the uninitiated, cataloging a sheet map, or map set/series, seems very daunting at first, what with things such as "scale," "projection," and "coordinates" to worry about, as well as "measuring between the neat lines." However, closer inspection reveals that the overall process of cataloging a map is not much more difficult than cataloging a basic monograph. It honestly is not more complicated, but it can be more complex because of the normal situation of having more than one title to choose from and also the physical features involved with sheet maps. If you place a blank workform for a map next to a blank workform for a monograph, you will find that only two fixed fields are different (Relief and Projection) between the two and one field (Index) is interpreted a little differently. In addition, three required coded variable fields are on the map workform (007, 034, and 052), but not on the monograph workform, along with one additional descriptive variable field, that being for the scale and other mathematical data, the 255 field. In all other instances the fields are the same between the two workforms, except that the workform for a monograph contains some differing fixed fields, such as "Biography."

A GOOD WAY TO BEGIN

All catalogers develop their own methodology to get the cataloging job done. Therefore, what I'm about to describe works well for me but may not for other catalogers. Still, I would like to share my approach toward cataloging the next map that comes off the "to be cataloged" shelf. Let me also share that after nearly fifteen years of cataloging primarily sheet maps I still fill out a paper workform before going online to complete the actual cataloging task on OCLC. Although some may find this method outdated and feel just as comfortable filling out the electronic workform on the OCLC site, I have found that cataloging first on paper serves as a way of double-checking my information between the time each piece of information is determined and entered on that sheet of paper until it is keyed into OCLC. Frequently, the task of keying the information into the online workform will trigger a mental reminder to double-check something as simple as the correct code for a fixed field, especially when I leave that field blank on the paper form. Another way of accomplishing the double-check when cataloging directly online is to put the completed workform in the online "Save file" and go back to it the next day. Whichever method is chosen, keeping the map being cataloged on hand until the task is completed ensures that all pieces of information are accounted for and allows one to go to the map to double-check accuracy of the transcription made to the bibliographic record.

It is very important to know all the little details of a particular map that one is about to catalog before starting the bibliographic description. I strongly recommend that for each title, depending on the complexity of the map(s) involved, at least two or three minutes be spent closely inspecting the map(s) and its (their) details. If you are new to cataloging maps, this process should take longer because of information that is there but hard to find or extrapolate; also, discovering which pieces of information are *not* on the item takes time to get to know, see, and comprehend.

This review process allows the cataloger to mentally check off some very important items relating to the map, both in terms of what is there and what is not. Details such as more than one possible title to choose from, whether a scale statement is available and in what form, publication information including dates, and the layout of the cartographic information, just to name a few, will give you a feel for what will be easy to transcribe into the record versus what is not there and/or will need more research before proceeding. It has also been my experience that *rarely* does any given map have all of the bibliographic details available; usually at least one aspect is lacking, such as scale, publication date, or a responsible person or party. So, once again, take the time to review the item in hand and mentally inventory what bibliographic information is readily available. The time spent will be well worth it in terms of providing a detailed and accurate bibliographic record.

My personal next step is to do any and all authority work necessary based on names of corporate bodies, individuals, and geographic areas involved. This tends to make the actual bibliographic description process go more smoothly and efficiently. Naturally, with time and experience, many of the corporate and geographic headings involved will become ingrained and you will not need to do as much authority checking, but even an experienced map cataloger takes the time to check anything he or she doubts.

Finally, once you have the "lay of the land" (pun intended) or a "feel" for the map, and the authority work completed so that you are ready to provide accurate headings, it is time to begin writing or keying the information from the map into the record. At this point, begin with whatever portion of the record with which you are most comfortable; for me, that tends to be the title and then the main entry. Before we proceed, however, let's look at the idea of "main map," or "main maps," as the case may be. This is part of seeing the big picture and goes hand in hand with the review process described previously.

THE CONCEPT OF "MAIN MAP"

Sheet maps come in many different sizes and "flavors," but before creating an accurate bibliographic description of the map, the cataloger must know and understand what he or she is describing. The simplest sheet map is one map printed on one side of one sheet of paper, but even this type may have one or more map insets and/or ancillary maps. In this particular case, there is only one main map to be described, and the gist of the bibliographic record that you are about to create must focus on that single main map. The concept of a "main map" flows from something we call publisher's intent; that is, based on both the content of the item in hand and, in large part, the title that it is given, is there rightfully only one primary map on the sheet, placing all other maps into a secondary or even tertiary role? A combination of close examination of the cartographic details plus careful consideration of the title(s) given on the item usually reveals a clear intent, including not only the subject content involved but also which is the main map, if more than one map is on the sheet.

Allow me at this point to define two terms—"inset maps," generically known as "insets," and "ancillary maps,"—before proceeding with other possible main map scenarios. In *Cartographic Materials: A Manual of Interpretation for AACR2* (CM), the definition of "inset" is "[a] separate map positioned within the neat line of a larger map." The definition for "ancillary map" is either "[a] small supplementary or secondary map outside the neat line of the principal or main map" or "[a] generic term for small supplementary or secondary maps located either inside or outside the neat line of the principal or main map" (Anglo-American Cataloguing Committee for Cartographic Material [AACCCM], 1982, pp. 229 and 223, respectively). The key difference between these two types of additional maps is the "supplementary or secondary" aspect denoted with the ancillary map. An ancillary map is an *additional* and usually *complementary* map that assists the main map in explaining a concept; for example, a map of volcanoes may have an ancillary map showing major earthquake epicenters to illustrate the relationship between the two geological events. An inset map is an *enlargement* of an area of the main map provided so that the map user can see details more explicitly. This is a commonly used technique on U.S. state highway maps, where individual cities appear as insets in the corners and/or on the verso side of the map. Another common application is when a map of a city includes an inset of the central part of the city, or the "central business district," again done to highlight the details of this geographic area of the city, such as historic or government buildings.

Lest you begin to believe that all maps have only one main map, let me assure you that this is not the case. A given work may have two, three, or more main maps, all on one sheet or on multiple sheets. In addition, these main maps may all be of the same geographic area, each with a different focus, or they may be of totally different areas. "Publisher's intent" is the key once again, and variety does complicate things in terms of providing an accurate physical description for the bibliographic record. I'll leave the physical description details to Chapter 13, which is devoted to the 300 field, but close with some examples of multiple main maps.

The American Automobile Association has been producing state highway maps for decades and sometimes will do so for two neighboring states. Such is the case for Alabama and Georgia, where the Library of Congress identifies these as "2 maps on 1 sheet" in the 300 field. This can be interpreted as "2 main maps on 1 sheet," but the "main" is implied in the Extent of item statement. See Figure 2.1 for the bibliographic record for this particular title. The rest of the Physical Description Area indicates that one of the main maps is on one side of the sheet and the second is on the other side by the use of "both sides."

Another example is of a recent tourist map of Montreal, Canada, that has what might be considered two main maps. Upon closer inspection, however, an area of the city map shows a box outlining a portion of the city, and a separate map of that section of the city appears on the other side of the sheet. Some catalogers may determine that each of these maps is a primary, or "main," map and describe the physical circumstances as "2 maps on 1 sheet : |b both sides . . ." But, using the title and statement of responsibility of the work for guidance, the primary map is of the city itself and the enlargement and several other maps are insets or ancillary maps. Figure 2.2 shows the bibliographic record for this title.

Sometimes it is difficult to ascertain which of multiple maps on one sheet are the main maps, especially when the item lacks a collective title and each of the maps has its own title. In addition, different catalogers will make different decisions regarding which is (are) the main map(s). A perfect example of this difference in interpretation involves the aforementioned Montreal tourist map. A title search for this map in OCLC will bring up three bibliographic records, one for the title in Figure 2.2 and two others of the same title but from other editions. The cataloger who created the record for the 2000-2001 edition of this map decided that there are eight main maps involved. Neither cataloger is "wrong" in this context; we simply saw the layout and publisher's intent in a different manner, and in each case, cataloger's judgment affected the outcome of the physical description.

One method of determining the main map or maps, especially when lacking a collective title for guidance, is first to identify and rule out all insets and ancillary maps. Once this has been done, the rest of the description falls into place. Figure 2.3 is a copy of a bibliographic record for one map that is more difficult to describe than most others due to the lack of a collective title and the multiple maps involved. Here, I had to use cataloger's judgment to decide whether this item had only one main map and multiple ancillary and inset maps or more than one main map. Ultimately, because the purpose of the

OCLC: 41966938   Rec stat: c
Entered: 19981221   Replaced: 20010701   Used: 20000316
Type: e   ELvl: Srce: Relf: bg   Ctrl: Lang: eng
BLvl: m   Form: GPub: SpFm: MRec: Ctry: flu
CrTp: a   Indx: 1   Proj: DtSt: s   Dates: 1996,
Desc: a
  1 010   98-678931
  2 040   DLC |c DLC |d OCL
  3 007   a |b j |d c |e a |f n |g z |h n
  4 034 1 a |b 906000
  5 034 1 a |b 887040
  6 045 0 |b d1997
  7 050 00 G3971.P2 1997 |b .A4
  8 052   3971
  9 052   3921
 10 072 7 P2 |2 lcg
 11 090 |b
 12 049   UPMM
 13 110 2 American Automobile Association.
 14 245 10 Alabama, Georgia.
 15 246 3 AAA Alabama, Georgia
 16 250   1997 ed.
 17 255   Scale 1:906,000. 1 in. = approx. 14 miles or 22.5 km.
 18 255   Scale [ca. 1:887,040]. 1 in. = approx. 14 miles or 23.0 km.
 19 260   Heathrow, FL : |b American Automobile Association, |c c1996.
 20 300   2 maps on 1 sheet : |b both sides, col. ; |c 60 x 58 cm., sheet 95 x
60 cm., folded to 23 x 10 cm.
 21 500   "96-10."
 22 500   Relief shown by shading and spot heights.
 23 500   Panel title.
 24 500   At head of panel title: AAA.
 25 500   Includes indexes, 19 local route maps, police emergency numbers,
distance map, and tourist information.
 26 505 0 Alabama -- Georgia.
 27 651 0 Alabama |v Road maps.
 28 651 0 Georgia |v Road maps.

FIGURE 2.1. American Automobile Association (AAA) Map of Alabama and
Georgia Bibliographic Record (*Source:* WorldCat Database, the OCLC Online
Union Catalog [WorldCat], see <http://www.oclc.org/firstsearch/database/details/
dbinformation_WorldCat.html>.)

OCLC: 47234141   Rec stat: n
Entered: 20010703   Replaced: 20010703   Used: 20010703
Type: e   ELvl: I   Srce: d   Relf: Ctrl: Lang: fre
BLvl: m   Form: GPub: I   SpFm: MRec: Ctry: quc
CrTp: a   Indx: 1   Proj: DtSt: t   Dates: 2001,1997
Desc: a
   1 040   UPM |c UPM
   2 007   a |b j |d c |e a |f n |g z |h n
   3 034 1   a |b 9504
   4 043   n-cn-qu
   5 052   3454 |b M8
   6 090   G3454.M8E635 2001 |b .M6
   7 090 |b
   8 049   UPMM
   9 245 00 Montráeal, 2001-2002 carte touristique officielle / ßc Tourisme Montráeal ;
Sociáetáe de transport de la Communautáe urbaine de Montráeal ; cartographie
numáerique, Gáeomatique, Ville de Montráeal, Dimension DPR inc.
   10 246 30 Montráeal, carte touristique officielle, 2001-2002
   11 246 1 |i Map title: |a Centre-ville = |b [City center]
   12 255   Scale [1:9,504]. 250 máetres = 0.15 miles.
   13 260   Montráeal : |b Cette carte est publiáee pour Tourisme Montráeal et la
Sociáetáe de transport de la Communautáe urbaine de Montráeal par les Publications
Touristiques LCR inc., |c 2001, c1997.
   14 300   1 map : |b col. ; |c 24 x 40 cm., folded to 23 x 8 cm.
   15 500   Panel title.
   16 500   "Informations repetoriáees en Janvier 2001."
   17 500   "[copyright] Ville de Montráeal, Service des travaux publics, 1997."
   18 500   Insets: Quartiers touristiques -- Parc Jean-Drapeau -- Est de l'Ile.
   19 500   Indexed for information kiosks, attractions, historic buildings and places,
churches, museums, parks, etc.
   20 500   Oriented with north to the upper right.
   21 500   Includes tourist information and col. advertisements.
   22 500   Ancillary and inset maps on verso: Vieux-Montráeal/Vieux-Port -- Ráeseau
piáetonnier souterrain -- Máetro -- Ráegion de Montráeal.
   23 500   Indexed ancillary and inset maps, tourist information, and col. advertisements
on verso.
   24 651 0   Montráeal (Quáebec) |v Maps, Tourist.
   25 650 0   Central business districts |z Quáebec (Province) |z Montráeal ßv Maps.
   26 650 0   Local transit |z Quáebec (Province) |z Montráeal |v Maps.
   27 650 0   Roads |z Quáebec (Province) |z Montráeal Region |v Maps.
   28 710 1   Montráeal (Quáebec). |b Gáeomatique.
   29 710 1   Montráeal (Quáebec). |b Service des travaux publics.
   30 710 2   Communautáe urbaine de Montráeal (Quáebec). |b Sociáetáe de transport.
   31 710 2   Tourisme Montráeal.
   32 710 2   Dimension DPR inc.
   33 710 2   Publications Touristiques LCR inc.

FIGURE 2.2. Montreal Tourist Map Bibliographic Record (*Source:* WorldCat
Database, the OCLC Online Union Catalog [WorldCat], see <http://www.oclc.
org/firstsearch/database/details/dbinformation_WorldCat.html>.)

OCLC: 47352854   Rec stat: n
Entered: 20010716   Replaced: 20010716   Used: 20010716
Type: e   ELvl: I   Srce: d   Relf: Ctrl: Lang: eng
BLvl: m   Form: GPub: SpFm: MRec: Ctry: pau
CrTp: a   Indx: 0   Proj: DtSt: s   Dates: 1999,
Desc: a

1	040	UPM |c UPM
2	007	a |b j |d c |e a |f n |g z |h n
3	034 0	a
4	043	n-us-pa
5	052	3822 |b L4
6	052	3824 |b A4
7	090	G3822.L4Q8 1999 |b .L4
8	090	|b
9	049	UPMM

10 245 04 The Lehigh Valley |h [map] : |b [First Union bank and ATM locations map]

11 255   Scale not given.

12 260   [Allentown, Pa.] : |b Lehigh Valley Convention & Visitors Bureau, |c c1999.

13 300   1 map : |b col. ; |c 38 x 28 cm., folded to 18 x 23 cm.

14 500   Shows First Union bank and ATM locations.

15 500   Panel title.

16 500   Indexed.

17 500   "[copyright] 1999 Lehigh Valley Convention & Visitors Bureau."

18 500   Includes insets of Kutztown and Lehigh Valley International Airport area.

19 500   Insets on verso: Route 22 Corridor -- Western Lehigh Valley -- Bethlehem -- Allentown -- Easton.

20 650 0 Banks and banking |z Pennsylvania |z Lehigh River Valley Region |v Maps.

21 650 0 Branch banks |z Pennsylvania |z Lehigh River Valley Region |v Maps.

22 650 0 Branch banks |z Pennsylvania |z Allentown Region |v Maps.

23 710 2 First Union National Bank of North Carolina.

24 710 2 Lehigh Valley Convention and Visitors Bureau.

FIGURE 2.3. Example of Difficult Main Map Situation, the "Lehigh Valley" Map Bibliographic Record (*Source:* WorldCat Database, the OCLC Online Union Catalog [WorldCat], see <http://www.oclc.org/firstsearch/database/details/dbinformation_WorldCat.html>.)

maps on the sheet was to show bank branch and ATM locations for one banking company scattered throughout a region in eastern Pennsylvania, I decided that the regional map was the primary one and based the rest of the description upon it, including using that regional map's title as the primary title.

As you go through the process of cataloging, make sure to take time to double-check anything about which you are uncertain. Soon, you will be comfortable with the process, and I'm sure that you will find working with such graphically oriented materials as maps more fun than cataloging most text-based materials!

Chapter 3

Necessary Tools of the Trade

Naturally, to do an adequate and accurate job of describing sheet maps we need to have a number of basic cataloging tools as well as some cartographic-specific ones. One should have a copy of the latest edition of AACR2R available as well as Library of Congress Subject Headings either in paper or electronic form. Also, if your institution uses the Library of Congress classification system, then you will need access to the paper or electronic Schedule G in order to build correct call numbers. The electronic form of the G-Schedule is found at the Library of Congress Classification Web and has links to the geographic area cutter tables, enabling one to retrieve both the classification number and, if needed, the geographic area cutter for a particular place.

BASIC CATALOGING TOOLS

Anglo-American Cataloguing Rules, Second Edition, 2002 Revision (AACR2R)
Library of Congress Rule Interpretations (LCRI)
Library of Congress Subject Cataloging Manual: Subject Headings (SCM)
Library of Congress Subject Headings (LCSH)
MARC 21 Concise Format for Bibliographic Data
MARC Code List for Geographic Areas
MARC Code List for Countries
Free-Floating Subdivisions: An Alphabetical Index
LC Period Subdivisions Under Names of Places

In addition, the following cartographic-specific essential and helpful tools are needed to complete the task at hand. Naturally, expect that some links for items found on the Web may no longer be accurate, but hopefully most or all changed links will have automatic forwarding capabilities to get you to the site that you are attempting to reach.

ESSENTIAL TOOLS

Available in Only Hard-Copy Form

- *Cartographic Materials: A Manual of Interpretation for AACR2.* Prepared by the Anglo-American Cataloguing Committee for Cartographic Materials. Chicago: American Libraries Association, 1982.

This text is out of print. The second edition is forthcoming in 2003.

- A "Natural Scale Indicator," created by Dr. Clifford Wood.

A plastic copy is available from:

Dr. Clifford Wood
Department of Geography
Memorial University of Newfoundland
St. John's, Newfoundland
Canada, A1B 3X9
E-mail: chwood@kean.ucs.mun.ca
Web site: <http://www.mun.ca/geog/resources/muncl/products/msi.htm>

Price is approximately $7.50 each. If you would rather save some dollars but not have as readable a product, paper versions of this tool are found in either of the following:

Boggs, Samuel Whittemore and Lewis, Dorothy Cornwell. *The Classification and Cataloging of Maps and Atlases.* New York: Special Libraries Association, 1963.

Foreign Maps. Washington, DC: U.S. Department of the Army, 1970. (Technical manual; TM 5-248)

A Must Have

- A tape measure or yardstick that has centimeters on it.

Available in Only Electronic Form

- GNIS Web site *(primary source for U.S. place names)* <http://geonames.usgs.gov/pls/gnis/web_query.gnis_web_query_form>
- GEOnet Names Server Web site *(primary source for international place names)* <http://gnpswww.nima.mil/geonames/GNS/index.jsp>
- Library of Congress Classification Web *(primary source for G-classification numbers and geographic area cutters)* <http://classweb.loc.gov/>

Available in Electronic and Hard-Copy Forms

- *Bibliographic Formats and Standards,* Second Edition. Columbus, OH: OCLC, 1993, 1996; <http://www.oclc.org/oclc/bib/about.htm>; ISBN 1-55653-216-4.
- *G: Geography, Maps, Anthropology, Recreation, Library of Congress Classification,* 2001 Edition. Washington, DC: Library of Congress, Cataloging Distribution Service, 2001; ISBN 0-8444-1040-3.

An alternative to LC's paper G-schedule is *Super LCCS: Gale's Library of Congress Classification Schedules Combined with Additions and Changes Through 1993: Class G, Geography; Maps; Anthropology; Recreation,* Rita Runchock and Kathleen Droste, editors. Detroit: Gale Research, Inc., 1994; ISBN 0-8103-8713-1. This is available on CD-ROM as *Super LCCS on CD.*

- "Classification Schedule G." In *Classification Plus.* Annual subscription. Washington, DC: Library of Congress Cataloging Distribution Service.

Otherwise known as the "Electronic G," or Library of Congress Schedule G, as part of the *Classification Plus* database software. As mentioned in the opening paragraph to this chapter, the "Electronic G" contains links from within the classification numbers to a separate set of geographic area cutter tables, enabling one to assemble both the classification number and the geographic area cutter in one easy step. And, the Library of Congress updates the geographic area cutter tables on a frequent basis. Finally, for the first time, one has a database of geographic area cutters that are worldwide in scope. This makes this tool the most powerful of the G-Schedules listed.

- LC Geography and Map Division's *Map Cataloging Manual.* Washington, DC: Cataloging Distribution Service, Library of Congress, 1991; ISBN 0-8444-0691-0; <http://www.tlcdelivers. com/tlc/crs/map0001.htm>.

Note: This is also available as part of the *Cataloger's Desktop* software package.

HELPFUL TOOLS

Available in Only Hard-Copy Form

Cataloging-Specific Tools

- *Maps and Related Cartographic Materials: Cataloging, Classification and Bibliographic Control,* Paige G. Andrew and Mary Lynette Larsgaard, co-editors. Binghamton, NY: The Haworth Press, Inc., 1999; ISBN 0-7890-0778-9 (hdbd.)/0-7890-0813-0 (pbk.).

This is copublished simultaneously as *Cataloging and Classification Quarterly,* 27(1/2, 3/4).

- *Notes in the Catalog Record: Based on AACR2 and LC Rule Interpretations,* by Jerry D. Saye and Sherry L. Vellucci. Chicago: American Library Association, 1989; ISBN 0-8389-3348-3.

Similar in nature to the following title except the book is arranged by type of note first, then subordered by the chapters that are from

AACR2R. I found this a more difficult approach to use when looking for notes specific to map cataloging.

- *Notes for Catalogers: A Sourcebook for Use with AACR2*, Florence A. Salinger and Eileen Zagon. White Plains, NY: Knowledge Industry Publications, 1984 (out of print); ISBN 0-86729-099-4 (hdbd.)/0-86729-098-6 (pbk.).

This publication showed me how to format different kinds of map-related notes. Many, many great examples of notes commonly used in the 500 fields are included, arranged by type of note, beginning with the "Nature and scope of the item" note and progressing through the other types of notes given in AACR2R.

- The LC Geography and Map Division's *Geographic Cutters,* Microfiche. Washington, DC: Cataloging Distribution Service, Library of Congress, 1988.

Note: This has become quite dated and, more important, *only covers geographic places in the United States.* This product is practically obsolete when compared to the new one containing the Geographic Cutters table—the new Library of Congress Classification Web site on the World Wide Web (http://classweb.loc.gov). However, if you do not have access to this site, you should continue to maintain a copy of this title available for use with U.S. place names.

- *Index to the Library of Congress "G" Schedule: A Map and Atlas Classification Aid.* ALA MAGERT Circular No. 2; ISBN 0-8389-7821-5.
- *National Geographic Desk Reference.* Washington, DC: National Geographic Society, 1999; ISBN 0-7922-7082-7 or 0-7922-7083-5 (deluxe).
- *OCLC Technical Bulletin 212* (field-specific format integration changes).

Note: This publication is no longer available in either hard-copy or electronic form. However, most cataloging department reference sections should contain a collection of OCLC technical bulletins, including this particular one.

Sources for Geographic Names

- *Rand McNally Commercial Atlas and Marketing Guide.* Chicago: Rand McNally (annual).
- *Merriam-Webster's New Geographical Dictionary,* Third Edition. Springfield, MA: Merriam-Webster, Inc., 1997.
- *Omni Gazetteer of the United States of America.* Detroit, MI: Omnigraphics, Inc., 1991.

Special Dictionaries

- *Dictionary of Geological Terms,* Third Edition, prepared under the direction of the American Geological Institute, Robert L. Bates and Julia A. Jackson, editors. New York: Doubleday, 1984; ISBN 0-385-18101-9.
- *Dictionary of Scientific and Technical Terms* or *McGraw-Hill Dictionary of Scientific and Technical Terms.* New York: McGraw-Hill Book Company, 1996; ISBN 0-07-042333-4.

Reference Atlases

- *National Geographic Atlas of the World,* Sixth Edition. Washington, DC: National Geographic Society, 1995; ISBN 0-87044-398-4.
- *Hammond World Atlas,* Ambassador Edition. Maplewood, NJ: Hammond, Inc., 1985; ISBN 0-8437-1242-2.
- *The Times Atlas of the World,* Tenth Edition. New York: Times Books Group, Ltd., 1999; ISBN 0-8129-3265-X.
- *World Mapping Today,* Second Edition, R. B. Parry and C. R. Perkins, editors. London: Bowker, Saur, 2000; ISBN 1-85739-035-0.

Available in Only Electronic Form

- WAML's "Map Librarian's Toolbox"
  <http://www.waml.org/maptools.html>
- MAGERT's "Electronic Publications" page
  <http://www.magert.whoi.edu:8000/elecpubs.htm>

- "Mathematical Data for Bibliographical Descriptions" site
  <http://www.konbib.nl/kb/resources/frameset_kb.html?/kb/skd/
  skd/mathemat.html>

This Web site was created, and is maintained, by Jan Smits, Map Curator at the Netherlands National Library, as a resource for anything to do with map scale, projections, coordinates, and equinox. Most helpful is the "Bar Scale Values" table for help in converting unusual/little-known scale systems to representative fractions; an area on geographic coordinates with links to other Web sites for more specific information on grid systems; and a list of prime meridians.

- Map Scale Indicator
  <http://www.mun.ca/geog/resources/muncl/products/msi.htm>
- Cataloging Calculator (Find G-Schedule classification numbers, subject codes, geographic area codes, and language codes.)
  <http://home.earthlink.net/banerjek/cutter.html>
- Scale Calculator (Plug in a distance and let this calculate the scale for you!)
  <http://ucs.orst.edu/~reeset/html/scale.html>
- Form/Genre Subject Headings/Subdivisions or "|v" Helpful Sites
  <http://www.lib.usm.edu/%7Etechserv/cat/formsubv.htm#top>
  <http://www.pitt.edu/~agtaylor/ala/edforum.htm>
- Reference Sources (dictionaries, glossaries, etc.)
  <http://www.geotech.org/survey/geotech/dictiona.html>
  <http://www.geology.iastate.edu/new_100/glossary.html>
- Selected Map Library Home Pages (with useful links to other sources of cartographic information)
  <http://www.lib.utexas.edu/maps/index.html> (Perry-Castañeda Library, University of Texas at Austin) (Here's where you can download those 8½-by-11-inch CIA maps.)
  <http://www-map.lib.umn.edu/map_libraries. phtml#organizations> (Borchert Map Library, University of Minnesota) (See the extensive list of Map Library Organizations!)
  <http://hcl.harvard.edu/maps/cart> (Harvard Map Library) (See the "Cartography Links" for links to a myriad of helpful sites.)
- Gateway to all things cartographic
  <http://oddens.geog.uu.nl/index.html> (Odden's bookmark is the most comprehensive Web site of its kind.)

Available in Electronic and Hard-Copy Forms

Sources for Geographic Names

- *Columbia Gazetteer of the World,* in three volumes. New York: Columbia University Press, 1998; <http://columbiagazetteer. org/>.

OCLC Technical Bulletins

- *OCLC Technical Bulletin 236* (updates to fixed field codes); <http://www.oclc.org/oclc/tb/tb236/index.htm>.

Chapter 4

Sources of Information

No matter the type of material, AACR2R tells us which part(s) of the item specific information must be taken from and, in certain parts of the record, the information that may also be taken from a secondary source. The Chief Source of Information for cartographic materials is specific, yet flexible, as it must be. Following Rule 3.0B2 for "Chief source of information" and Rule 3.0B3 for "Prescribed sources of information" allows the cataloger to determine where information can be derived from to go into the bibliographic record and when information must be bracketed because it comes from outside of the Prescribed sources of information.

CHIEF SOURCE OF INFORMATION

Rule 3.0B2 states that any part of the map and/or its container can be used in determining what information can go into the record, and if information is not found in either of these places, then the cataloger can take information from accompanying printed material and use it in the record (see Figure 4.1). Notice that this is broader in context than the Chief source of information for monographs, which specifies that information must come from "the title page, or, if there is no title page, the source from within the publication that is used as a substitute for it."

This can be very fortunate when it comes to sheet maps, as it allows the range of flexibility sometimes needed when cataloging maps. For example, this flexibility is apparent in terms of using a title from a container as opposed to from a map when the title on the map is less comprehensive than that on the container or when a title is not found on the map. Yet this same flexibility means that we must be alert to pertinent information coming from just about anywhere on the map or its con-

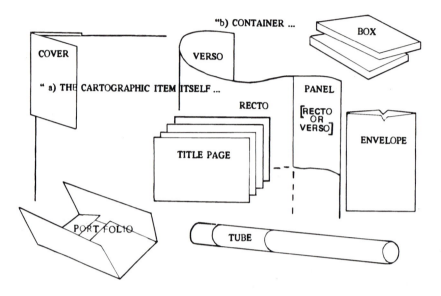

FIGURE 4.1. Chief Source of Information (*Source:* Reproduced from *Cartographic Materials: A Manual of Interpretation for the AACR2,* 1982, p. 8. Permission granted by the American Library Association.)

tainer, meaning more diligence and potentially more work on our part. In contrast, someone cataloging a monograph, in the majority of cases, has to use only the title page and its verso to derive most of the bibliographic information needed to complete a record. This is why it is important to spend some time looking over and analyzing all of the information found on a map before beginning the cataloging process, as mentioned previously in Chapter 2.

PRESCRIBED SOURCES OF INFORMATION

For each area of the bibliographic record, Rule 3.0B3 specifies where information may be taken from in order to be placed in the record. In most cases, such as the "Title and statement of responsibility area," this is the Chief source of information and/or accompanying printed material for sheet maps. The "Physical description area," "Note area," and "Standard number and terms of availability area" all list "Any source" as the Prescribed sources of information, thereby allowing the cataloger the option of considering all available sources for these areas, such as other reference works (see Table 4.1).

Note once again that if information is derived from outside of the Prescribed sources of information for each of the areas listed in Rule 3.0B3, except for those denoted as "Any source", then it must be given in square brackets in the record to indicate that the cataloger found the given information in a source other than the map itself or its container.

TABLE 4.1. Rule 3.0B3. Prescribed Sources of Information for Each Area of the Description for Cartographic Materials

Area	Prescribed Sources of Information
Title and statement of responsibility	Chief source of information
Edition	Chief source of information, accompanying printed material
Mathematical data	Chief source of information, accompanying printed material
Publication, distribution, etc.	Chief source of information, accompanying printed material
Physical description	Any source
Series	Chief source of information, accompanying printed material
Note	Any source
Standard number and terms of availability	Any source

Note: Enclose information taken from outside the prescribed source(s) in square brackets.

SECTION II:
CODED FIELDS

Chapter 5

Cartographic-Specific Fixed Fields

This chapter focuses on the small number of fixed fields that pertain uniquely to cartographic items and, in one case, a fixed field that is interpreted differently but is also used for other kinds of materials. The unique fields include the "Type of Cartographic Material," "Relief," and "Projection" fixed fields. The "Type of Record" fixed field occurs in all records but is coded uniquely to indicate the type of material being cataloged. The fixed field which occurs in a number of other format-specific bibliographic records but which is interpreted differently is the "Index" fixed field. All of the other fixed fields involved, by and large, can be found in a record for monographs and are coded the same or similarly; these are addressed in the next chapter.

- *Type of Record (Type):* Mandatory. Although this fixed field is not unique to cartographic materials, the code provided is. This is where the code for type of material is placed, and the code for cartographic materials is "e".
- *Type of Cartographic Material (CrTp):* Mandatory. This fixed field is coded to show the specific type of cartographic material being cataloged, such as map, atlas, or globe. For sheet maps this is coded "a".
- *Relief (Relf):* Mandatory. Early in the history of cartography, mapmakers discovered that they needed to employ one or more graphical means to show elevation above the surface of the Earth, and later depths below the surface of our oceans or other bodies of water. Each of the artistic means of showing elevation and depth, and later also mathematical means, has a name, and each of these names is given in coded form in this fixed field. The cataloger can employ up to four codes in the field, although often only one or two means of relief are shown on the map. Also, in those cases in which combinations of elevation and depth shown can provide more than

four types of relief, the cataloger must choose which ones to code in the field, usually by trying to determine those which are the most prominently shown. A table of codes for relief types is found with the "Relief" fixed field chapter in OCLC's *Bibliographic Formats and Standards* and also in the *MARC 21 Concise Format for Bibliographic Data*.

The most common method of showing relief in elevation is by the use of contours, coded "a", and spot heights, coded "g". In the eighteenth, nineteenth, and early twentieth centuries, a technique known as hachuring was widely used to show mountain peaks, mountain ranges, or both. One cartographer in particular became known for his precision and detail in using this method, and Erwin Raisz's maps are today known generically as Raisz maps because of his distinctive style. The presence of hachures on a map is coded "d" in the record. Use the table of codes to appropriately fill out this field. For visual assistance as to what each relief type looks like on a map, there is a plate in *Cartographic Materials* between pages 150 and 151 specifically designed and included for this purpose.

- *Projection (Proj):* Required if applicable. This field employs a two-letter code to identify the type of projection used to make the map and must also be given in its textual, or word, form in subfield "b" of the 255 field. If a 255 |b exists then the cataloger must code this fixed field. Once again, a table of projection codes that covers everything from Mercator to Alber's equal area to Butterfly is given in OCLC's *Bibliographic Formats and Standards* at <http://www.oclc.org/oclc/bib/proj.htm> and in the *MARC 21 Concise Format for Bibliographic Data* at <http://lcweb.loc.gov/marc/bibliographic/ecbd008s.html#mrcb008p>; click on "008--Maps" and scroll down to "22-23 – Projection." If a particular projection stated on the map *is not* specifically listed with a code in the table, then use "zz" for "Other."

- *Index (Indx):* Optional. Code as "0" (zero) if there is not an index that shows a one-to-one correlation of items listed in the index to their locations on the map or not a separate gazetteer on or accompanying the map; code as "1" if there is an index or gazetteer available.

Chapter 6

General Fixed Fields

Note that the following list follows the order that the fixed fields are displayed on a bibliographic record or a blank OCLC workform for a cartographic material item, reading from top to bottom, starting with the lefthand column of labels and progressing to the right, skipping "Type" and the four other fixed fields noted in the previous chapter.

- *Bibliographic Level (BLvl):* Mandatory. Code as "m" for monographic titles and "s" for serial titles.
- *Descriptive Cataloging Form (Desc):* Mandatory. Code as "a" for AACR2R-level cataloging.
- *Encoding Level (Elvl):* Mandatory. Code as "I" for full-level cataloging, "k" for minimal-level cataloging. See OCLC's *Bibliographic Formats and Standards* for a complete explanation on what must be included in the record for each cataloging level and what other cataloging level codes mean.
- *Form of Item (Form):* Required if applicable. Leave blank for sheet maps unless the map is specifically published as a large-print item, the map is in Braille, or the map is a photocopy reproduction.
- *Cataloging Source Code (Srce):* Mandatory. Code as "d" to show that the record was created by a cataloger from an OCLC member institution. Bibliographic records with this fixed field coded "blank" are from national agencies; in the United States this would be the Library of Congress, and this applies for other country agencies, such as the National Library of Canada.
- *Government Publication (GPub):* Mandatory. See OCLC's *Bibliographic Formats and Standards* for a list of possible codes and their meanings. In most instances this fixed field will be coded "l" (letter "ell", not the number "one") for "Local government agency

publication"; "s" for "State government agency publication" (including public universities); and "f" for "Federal or National government agency publication".

- *Special Format Characteristics (SpFm):* Mandatory. See OCLC's *Bibliographic Formats and Standards* for a list of possible codes and their meanings. In the case of paper sheet maps, this will almost always be coded "blank" but should be coded "o" for wall maps, such as those mounted on rollers or those which have metal or plastic grommets or rings for the purpose of mounting on a wall. Other possibilities are given in the list of codes. You may provide up to two codes in this fixed field.

- *Type of Date/Publication Status (DtSt):* Mandatory. In the majority of cases, this fixed field will be coded "s" for "Single publication date," including a single copyright date or an uncertain date for a single year. By uncertain date this means that the date given in the 260 |c subfield is in square brackets, with or without a question mark. However, frequently the cataloger will need to supply an inferred date for a range of dates, and in these cases this field should be coded "q".

  Be aware that you may have to use code "t" for maps that have both a publication and a copyright date; "m" for map sets or series in which the individual sheets have been published over a range of years; and "r" for maps that are republications/published earlier or facsimiles of earlier maps.

- *Type of Control (Ctrl):* Required if applicable. The code for this fixed field indicates whether or not the item is under archival control, i.e., has been described using archival descriptive rules. If you are cataloging sheet maps in an archival setting, code "a" would apply, but for all other map collections, this fixed field is coded "blank".

- *Modified Record (MRec):* Required if applicable. This fixed field applies to sheet maps only when modifying an existing bibliographic record, for instance, if one were to romanize a record that had been created using a nonromanized script. Leave this as "blank" for creating most sheet map records, but use "o" when transliterating a title.

- *Date(s) of Publication (Date):* Mandatory. If the map was published in a single year then the first or left space will have the applicable four-digit year. If the DtSt fixed field is coded "q", "t", "m", or "r", then both sets of blanks will need to be filled with either four-digit beginning and ending years or digits for portions of a year plus the letter "u", which acts as a "filler" for an unknown year or decade, or all "u"s in one set of dates for an unknown year.

- *Language Code (Lang):* Mandatory. Use a three-letter code for this fixed field for the primary language used on the map; most of the time this will be "eng" for English. See the *MARC 21 Code List for Languages* to obtain codes for other languages.

- *Country of Publication, etc. (Ctry):* Required if applicable. For places of publication given in subfield "a" of the 260 field that are located in the United States or are one of the countries in the United Kingdom, you will supply a three-letter code. In the case of places in the United States, this code is at the state level; e.g., the code "pau" is for a place of publication in Pennsylvania or the code "nyu" is for a place of publication in the state of New York. Notice that this is a combination of the two-letter abbreviation for the state plus the letter "u" representing "United States."

For all other places of publication in other countries, this will be a two-letter code, e.g., "fr" for a place of publication in France or "sa" for a place of publication in South Africa. To find the appropriate code for this fixed field use the "Country of Publication Codes" list found in the *MARC 21 Code List for Countries,* found at <http://www.loc.gov/marc/countries/cntrhome.html> or by going to the MARC 21 home page at <http://lcweb.loc.gov/marc/> and clicking on the "Country" link under the MARC 21 Code Lists header. To determine other specific codes for special situations, such as when no place of publication is given or when a map has been published in more than one place, see OCLC's *Bibliographic Formats and Standards*.

Chapter 7

Coded Variable Fields

Coded variable fields used in the bibliographic record, such as the 007 field, or "Physical Description Fixed Field" for maps, serve to provide descriptive information in a coded form. The coded form of information makes machine-retrievable protocols possible in the electronic environment. That doesn't necessarily mean that existing coded fields are used in this manner by Integrated Library Systems or even homegrown electronic systems, but they are placed in the record for this purpose. For instance, I am not aware of any system that uses the 043 Geographic Area Code field in terms of online retrieval, but the alphabetic codes are available for use in this manner. In addition, you will find that coded variable fields have parallels to other descriptive variable fields in most instances. The most obvious of these pairings is the 034 and 255 fields; the denominator of the scale and the mathematical form of the coordinates are placed in the 034 field and the verbal form of the scale statement and coordinates are placed in the 255 field. Naturally, wherever a coded field is the match of a descriptive field, the information in both fields must be identical.

This chapter is divided between those coded fields which must be included in a full-level bibliographic record or included when the necessary information is available on the map and those coded fields which are optional and can be included at the discretion of the cataloger. If a particular field is repeatable, this is also indicated.

MANDATORY CODED FIELDS
FOR CARTOGRAPHIC MATERIALS

Four coded variable fields typically are used in the creation of a bibliographic record for a sheet map, three of which are mandatory in OCLC. The three mandatory fields are the 007 for coding the physical aspects of the map (which, at the time of this writing, may become optional), the 034 for showing scale and coordinate information in coded form, and the 052, which includes the classification number and, if applicable, the geographic area cutter, which are culled from the call number. The fourth field that can be used is the 043 field, optional in OCLC, that shows geographic location in coded form. The 043 field will be discussed later with other optional coded variable fields. Lists of codes and their meanings are found in OCLC's *Bibliographic Input Standards* and also in *MARC 21 Concise Format for Bibliographic Data* for the 007, 041, and 043 fields.

007 Field (Repeatable)

The "Coded Physical Description", or 007 field, is mandatory in OCLC for sheet maps and globes. This field provides a list of physical components of the map based on codes established for each of seven subfields. Each subfield, naturally, has a specific meaning and a set of codes to be used within that particular subfield. The coded information also must match the descriptive information found in subfields "a" and "b" in the Physical Description, or 300 field. Subfields "f" for "Type of production", "g" for "Production/reproduction details", and "h" for "Positive/negative aspect" are coded as "n" for "not applicable" or "z" for "other" for most basic sheet maps. For instance, when a blue-line print map is being cataloged, then these three subfields are coded appropriately and provide meaning for this particular physical form.

The most common set of 007 codes is for a colored map on paper and for a single-color (most often black-and-white but not always necessarily the case—more on this in Chapter 13) map on paper. After coding for these two typical situations for a period of time, the codes become ingrained in memory like a catchy ditty that sticks in your mind! A colored paper map is always "a, j, c, a, n, z, n" and a single-color paper map is always "a, j, a, a, n, z, n." Say each of these a few times out loud and you'll begin to pick up the "tune."

Colored map on paper:
007   a |b j |d c |e a |f n |g z |h n
300   1 map : |b col. ; |c 50 x 80 cm.

Uncolored (single-color) map on paper:
007   a |b j |d a |e a |f n |g z |h n
300   1 map ; |c 50 x 80 cm.

Other codes for specific physical characteristics of maps include the following:

Blue-line print (uncolored positive photocopy):
007   a |b j |d a |e a |f z |g a |h a
300   1 map : |b photocopy ; |c 50 x 80 cm.

Black-line print (dark lines on light/white background):
007   a |b j |d a |e a |f z |g b |h a
300   1 map : |b photocopy ; |c 50 x 80 cm.

Uncolored negative photocopy (light/white lines on dark [blue or black usually] background):
007   a |b j |d a |e a |f z |g b |h b
300   1 map : |b photocopy ; |c 50 x 80 cm.
500   Negative.

Uncolored facsimile map on paper:
007   a |b j |d a |e a |f f |g z |h n
300   1 map ; |c 50 x 80 cm.
500   Facsimile.

Colored facsimile map on paper:
007   a |b j |d c |e a |f f |g z |h n
300   1 map : |b col. ; |c 50 x 80 cm.
500   Facsimile.

Uncolored map on cloth:
007   a |b j |d a |e g |f n |g z |h n
300   1 map : |b on cloth ; |c 50 x 80 cm.

Colored map on cloth:
007   a |b j |d c |e g |f n |g z |h n
300   1 map : |b col., on cloth ; |c 50 x 80 cm.

034 Field (Repeatable)

The "Coded Mathematical Data" field, as mentioned previously, contains information in coded form which matches that found in descriptive form in the 255 field. When you are done coding this field, it is always wise to double-check the information you have keyed into the field with information in the 255 field, and if discrepancies are found, then they can be corrected. If necessary, whenever a discrepancy is found, it is best to go back to the map being cataloged to verify the accuracy of the information given in the 255 field, and then the 034 field can also be verified. (See Figure 11.4 for comparative sets of 255 and 034 fields.)

A complicating factor in applying this field is that subfield "a" is mandatory in all cases and "b" is mandatory when applicable, i.e., when a representative fraction is given in the 255 field. The four other subfields, for coordinate information, are optional if coordinates are not provided in the 255 field. Long-time Library of Congress cataloging practice is to provide coordinates when they exist on the map being cataloged but not provide them when it would take additional time to research an accurate set of bounding coordinates. This reflects the reality in which we all are working: Is the time taken to provide coordinates for a given map worth it in terms of patron need and access? After all, time *is* money, and therefore these kinds of situations must be looked at closely in terms of value provided. Until recently, the straightforward answer to the previous question was for the most part "No." However, beginning with the Alexandria Digital Initiative (ADI) project's database search capabilities and now with Endeavor's Voyager product, retrieving cartographic titles based on doing searches of bounding coordinates has become a powerful tool, and perhaps we need to rethink coordinate information as being optional as opposed to required. The following descriptions to applying the field are based on current rules and applications, but keep in mind that in the not too distant future coordinate application may change.

The indicator value for this field (0, 1, or 3 in the first indicator position; the second indicator position is always blank) is the key to what will appear in the remainder of the field. In all cases subfield "a" must appear in the field. In cases where no scale is on the map, three or more scales are involved with multiple maps, or in that rare instance of scale varying within one map (i.e., when one applies "Scale not given", "Not drawn to scale", "Scales differ", or "Scale varies", in the 255 field), the indicator value is "0" and therefore no subfield "b" will appear. However, one may provide coordinate values in subfields "d", "e", "f", and "g" even when subfield "b" is not present.

In all cases where one or two scales are provided on the map(s), the indicator value is "1" and a subfield "b" will exist in the field. Subfield "b" contains the denominator value(s) given in subfield "a" of the 255 field and is repeatable for up to two of these subfields. Again, if coordinates are provided in the 255 field, then they must also appear in the 034 field in their coded form.

In the specific case in which scale varies within one map and the scales are given, the indicator value is "3" and two subfield "b"s appear in the 034 field, one for each denominator of the scales given. And, in the case where both horizontal and vertical scales are given, the indicator value is "1" but the denominator of the vertical scale is placed in a subfield "c".

Finally, whereas a comma appears in the denominator value of the representative fraction in the 255 field, do not use a comma within this same value as it appears in subfield "b" or "c" of the 034 field.

052 Field (Repeatable)

The information appearing in this field is the classification number from the Library of Congress G-Schedule and, when applicable, the geographic area cutter. The classification number goes in subfield "a" and the geographic area cutter goes in subfield "b" of this field. Geographic area cutters are located in table form within the electronic version of the G-Schedule, on a Web site titled "Geographic Web." *Note:* Never place a *subject code* from the tables in the G-Schedule in this area. Examples of a variety of 052 classification numbers, with and without geographic area cutters, are as follows:

052   3920 (for a general map of Georgia)
052   3921 (for a topical map of Georgia)
052   3922 |b C6 (for a general map of the coast of Georgia)
052   3923 |b C5 (for a general map of Clarke County, Georgia)
052   3924 |b A7 (for a general map of Athens, Georgia)

In addition, the 052 field is repeatable, so that whenever you have more than one main map, you can code this field for each of the main maps involved. This means that if you have two main maps on one sheet, one of which is for a county and the other for the primary city within that county, you would provide one 052 code for the county involved and a second 052 code for the city involved. For example:

052   3823 |b C4 (for Centre County, Pennsylvania)
052   3824 |b B37 (for Bellefonte, Pennsylvania)

Also, subfield "b" within the 052 field is repeatable. This is so that you can code for multiple regions, counties, or cities within each of these kinds of maps. For instance, if you have a map with multiple cities on it, each of these cities can be coded using the geographic area cutter. For example:

052   3824 |b B37 |b B628 |b L47 |b P52 |b P56

In this case, the map includes the cities of Bellefonte, Boalsburg, Lemont, Philipsburg, and Pine Grove Mills, Pennsylvania.

CODED VARIABLE FIELDS THAT ARE REQUIRED WHEN APPLICABLE

Other fields that are applied when necessary because the information that goes into them is available to the cataloger include the 020, 041, and 086 fields.

020 Field (Repeatable, Mandatory When Applicable)

In those cases in which an International Standard Book Number (ISBN) is present on the map, that number goes in the 020 field. If a retail price is available on the map, optionally, this information belongs in subfield "c".

041 Field (Not Repeatable, Mandatory When Applicable)

Whenever multiple languages are present on the map supply the coded form for languages in the 041 field and describe which languages are used where on the map in the 546 field. For example:

041   enggeritaspa
546   Place names on the map in English. Title and legend in
       English, German, Italian, and Spanish.

086 Field (Repeatable, Mandatory When Applicable)

For those maps with a Superintendent of Documents (SuDoc) number, most usually those obtained as part of the federal Depository Library Program, supply the SuDoc number in this field when known or available.

OPTIONAL CODED FIELDS
FOR CARTOGRAPHIC MATERIALS

In addition to the required coded variable fields, other coded fields can be used depending on circumstances. These include the 006 for bringing out noncartographic physical aspects of the item, e.g., a map that has a poster on the verso and thus could be more appropriately described as a nonprojected graphic item, as is the case with some National Geographic Society titles, or as in the case of a title from the Quebec Ministry of Natural Resources, a poster that is cartographic in nature and thus has been cataloged as a sheet map, titled "Parcourir le relief du Quebec!" (see Figure 7.1).

Other coded variable fields typically used in map cataloging that are optional include the 037 for stock numbers, the 045 for the time period shown on the map, and the 072 for providing other subject categories in coded form. Naturally, an appropriate call number field (090 or 099) can also be provided, but this is optional.

037 Field (Repeatable)

This field is used for company or agency product stock numbers. In addition, subfields are also employed to provide information as to the name of the company or agency that provided the stock number, terms of availability, additional format characteristics, and helpful notes.

OCLC: 47250608   Rec stat: c
Entered: 20010706   Replaced: 20010813   Used: 20010706
Type: e   ELvl: I   Srce: d   Relf: cg   Ctrl: Lang: fre
BLvl: m   Form: GPub: s   SpFm: MRec: Ctry: quc
CrTp: a   Indx: 0   Proj: DtSt: s   Dates: 2001,
Desc: a
 1 040   UPM |c UPM
 2 006   [k   s   in]
 3 007   a |b j |d c |e a |f n |g z |h n
 4 034 1 a |b 2300000 |d W0800000 |e W0560000 |f N0650000 |g N0450000
 5 043   n-cn-qu
 6 052   3451
 7 090   G3451.C2 2001 |b .Q4
 8 090 |b
 9 049   UPMM
10 110 1 Quáebec (Province). |b Ministáere des ressources naturelles.
11 245 10 Parcourir le relief du Quáebec! |h [map] / |c producteur, Ministáere
des Ressources naturelles du Quáebec ; collaborateur, Ministáere de
l'Environnement du Quáebec.

FIGURE 7.1. Example of 006 Field Usage (*Source:* WorldCat Database, the
OCLC Online Union Catalog [WorldCat], see <http://www.oclc.org/firstsearch/
database/details/dbinformation_WorldCat.html>.)

043 Field (Not Repeatable, but Subfields Repeatable with Limitations)

As mentioned earlier, the 043 field is often put in the record for
sheet maps, but it is an optional field and therefore local practice dictates whether it will be used. For instance, the Library of Congress
once used the 043 field for atlases but in recent years dropped the 043
field in favor of using the 052 field. This field contains one, two, or
three geographic area codes for countries; some first-order political
entities, e.g., states in the United States; large regional areas; continents; and geographic features found in MARC 21's *MARC Code
List for Geographic Areas,* at <http:// lcweb.loc.gov/marc/geoareas>
or in hard copy form. An alphabetic code is seven characters in
length, in the form of x-xx-xx, and when the code has fewer than five
letters the spaces are filled using additional dashes. Each code represents a single place.

045 Field (Nonrepeatable)

The "Coded Chronology" field is used to specify a point in time or range of years as depicted on the map. A 500 note providing descriptive information should also be given in the record.

072 Field (Repeatable)

The 072 field is a coded form of subject access for both subject terms and subject subdivisions. If a map is primarily about one topic but also includes one or more other appropriate topics, the cataloger can provide not only additional subject headings and/or subdivisions to bring out these secondary aspects of the map but also one or more matching 072 fields. Contents of the field include the alphanumeric subject code, taken from the subject lists in the G-Schedule.

090 Field (Repeatable)

This is the locally assigned LC-type call number field. Most usually maps are given call numbers based on the Library of Congress G-Schedule, but other LC call numbers may also go into this field, especially if the cataloging agency prefers to classify part of or all of a map collection according to subject area first.

099 Field (Repeatable)

Assign local free-text call numbers using this field. This would include well-known map classification schemes such as Boggs and Lewis's or the American Geographical Society's (AGS). For example, an AGS call number would appear as:

099 _ 9   050 B-2001

050 = world map
B   = historical or political, including archaeology, designation
2001 = in this case, year of publication

for the July 2001 National Geographic Society map "Treasures of the world, lost-and-found" (see OCLC# 47624894), if they had cataloged the map, or:

099 _ 9   813-d .S2F7 D-1943

813   = the classification number for California
-d   = city designator
.S2F7 = the cutter for San Francisco
D   = transportation/communication topics, including postal
        service
-1943 = the situation and publication date

for a 1943 map titled "Postal districts, San Francisco, California"
(see OCLC# 47642572).

SECTION III:
DESCRIPTION OF THE MAP

Chapter 8

Main Entry and Statement of Responsibility

Contemporary maps and atlases, those created from the midnineteenth century and later, typically are produced by government agencies or private companies. That said, it is understood that one or more individuals actually do the cartographic work involved. However, the cartographer(s), or combination of persons who actually create the map, the "author" of the map it could be said, usually is not named on the majority of those maps produced in this country or in others. Rather, recognition in the form of a statement of responsibility, when it is provided, is given to the company or agency "formally" named on the map. This is a major departure from most monographs, for which the individual(s) responsible for the work is (are) usually named as author of the work.

MAIN ENTRY UNDER PERSONAL AUTHOR

The Basic Rule area of Chapter 21 in AACR2R outlines the process of determining which of three possibilities for access to a work may be used: personal name, corporate body, or title. First, Rule 21.1A2 tells us to

> Enter a work by one or more persons under the heading for the personal author (see 21.4A), the principal personal author (see 21.6B), or the probable personal author (see 21.5B). In some cases of shared personal authorship (see 21.6) and mixed personal authorship (see 21.8-21.27), enter under the heading for the person named first. Make added entries as instructed in 21.29-21.30.

Note that in Rule 21.1A1 a definition for "personal author" is given, stating that "[a] personal author is the person chiefly responsible for the creation of the intellectual or artistic content of the work." This is all well and good, except for the circumstance mentioned in the introduction to this chapter, and that is that the majority of maps do not explicitly name an individual as being "responsible for the creation of the intellectual . . . content of the work."

However, if an individual *is* formally named as being responsible for the map (see the later section Terms That Indicate Responsibility for a Map for guidance), even if one or more corporate bodies are also prominently named, be sure to make the main entry for that named person. Or, if a person's name is part of the title of the map but this person is not formally named elsewhere, consider this a formal statement of responsibility as outlined in Rule 1.1F13 and enter the person's name as the main entry. If an individual is not named as being responsible for the map, then we must look at the next part of the Basic Rule, i.e., when to enter the map under corporate body.

MAIN ENTRY UNDER CORPORATE BODY

Unfortunately, in *Anglo-American Cataloguing Rules,* Second Edition (AACR2), published in 1978, Chapter 21, "Choice of Access Points," did not include in its list of types of corporate bodies under which main entry was allowed a section on those for maps. Rule 21.1B2 in AACR2 stated, "[e]nter a work emanating[2] from one or more corporate bodies under the heading for the appropriate corporate body if it falls into one or more of the following categories: . . ." but the five categories listed did not include cartographic materials. (We'll deal with "emanating" and its meaning shortly.) This meant that if a person was not named as the author of the map, then the primary access point was by title.

This situation simply did not allow for what was a reality with the vast majority of maps. We know that with contemporary maps attribution of responsibility most usually is given to a company or government agency. Therefore, the lack of an explicit category in 21.1B2 among those categories for corporate bodies meant that many maps were being cataloged using the title as the main entry. Or, when it was clear that mixed or shared responsibility for the production of the map was involved, either an individual or, in certain cases, a corporate body was given main entry status. Those were the choices left for the cataloger at that time.

The map librarianship community simply could not live with rules that did not allow the cataloger to provide main entry status for such common and well-known map producers as the Rand McNally Company or the U.S. Geological Survey. During the process to update AACR2, representatives from the Library of Congress and the various Anglo-American cartographic associations made it clear that a change to the rules was needed to rectify the existing situation. As a result, a final category was listed in Rule 21.1B2, that being category "f", which first appeared as a formal instruction in the *Library of Congress Cataloging Service Bulletin* (CSB), No. 14, Fall 1981 edition, as a revision to Rule 21.1B2. The CSB version states, "f) cartographic materials emanating from a corporate body other than a body that is responsible solely for the publication and distribution of the material." This was also incorporated into *Cartographic Materials,* published in 1982, as Appendix A, which included a valuable explanation of the decisions needed to determine corporate main entries for maps. Once published in AACR2R in 1988, the wording changed slightly to read, ". . . other than a body that is merely responsible for their publication or distribution." This finally allowed catalogers to apply main entry headings that parallel real-world circumstances. But what should you do if neither a personal name nor corporate body is given as being responsible for the map?

MAIN ENTRY UNDER TITLE

Rule 21.1C1 outlines four circumstances in which the cataloger must provide main entry by the title of a work. The second circumstance, the work "is a collection or a work produced under editorial direction" might apply to cataloging maps but under rare circumstances. The fourth circumstance might never apply to maps as it talks about works that are "accepted as sacred scripture by a religious group." However, the first and third circumstances do apply to maps.

The first circumstance in the rule is the one that most often means that a map is given title main entry status: "the personal authorship is unknown (see 21.5) or diffuse (see 21.6C2), and the work does not emanate from a corporate body." The first and third parts of this statement are straightforward, but "diffuse" must be understood in order to apply this rule. Rule 21.6C2 explains that diffuse means four or more persons or corporate bodies are named in the statement of responsibility as playing a role in the creation of a work, and principal responsibility is not attributed to any one, two, or three of these. In such a case, title main entry applies.

The third circumstance, "it emanates from a corporate body but does not fall into any of the categories given in 21.1B2 and is not of personal authorship," could possibly apply but likely would not happen with a map, since corporate bodies associated with a map usually play an "emanating" role and may be considered to fall into category "f" in 21.1B2.

"EMANATING FROM" AND ITS RELATIONSHIP TO THE STATEMENT OF RESPONSIBILITY

Another important aspect of the revision to Rule 21.1B2, published in the Fall 1981 CSB, is the interpretation of the phrase "emanate from." The discussion was presented in three steps and those are given in Box 8.1. This further gave recognition to the circumstances surrounding the entities typically involved with the creation of cartographic materials. A corporate body is often named as the responsible party on the map, explicitly or implicitly, and so part (f) was added to rule 21.1B2 for choosing a corporate body as the main entry for cartographic materials. It specifies that "cartographic materials emanating[2] from a corporate body" permits corporate body main entry in the bibliographic record. Footnote 2 for this rule explains what "emanating" means in this case: "Consider a work to have emanated from a corporate body if it is issued by that body *or* has been caused to be issued by that body *or* if it originated with that body."

Using the agency that produces the largest number of maps in the United States as an example, if the statement of responsibility reads "mapped, edited, and produced by the United States Geological Survey," then the main entry will be:

110   2   Geological Survey (U.S.)

because the map "emanates" from this agency, no matter how many unnamed individuals played a role in the production and outcome of

BOX 8.1. What "Emanating from" Means in Rule 21.1B2

"a) The corporate body has issued (published) the work. Normally this means that the name of the corporate body appears in a position indicative of publication (e.g., for books, the imprint position) in the chief source of information or appears elsewhere as a formal publication statement.

b) Corporate body A has caused the work to be issued (published). Generally, the name of a different body, corporate body B, appears on the chief source of information (cf. above) or elsewhere as a formal publisher statement. [In other words] body A has arranged for body B, named as publisher, to issue the work because body A has no facilities for publishing. The arrangement between the two bodies is in some cases explicitly stated, e.g., "Published for the Historical Association by Routledge & Paul." In other cases it must be inferred from evidence in the publication. For example, the name of body A at head of title . . . commonly indicates that body A has caused the item to be issued (published), or, if the work appears in a series for which body A has editorial responsibility but is published by a commercial publisher, body A has caused the work to be issued (published).

c) The corporate body, although the originator of the work, does not meet the test of issuing (publishing) in either category a) or b) above. In this case, body B, which has no responsibility for the content, issues (publishes) a work whose content originates with body A. For example, a work is prepared by corporate body A which functions as a consulting body, commissioned by body B for that purpose; the completed work is published by body B. In this case the content of the work originates with body A although it has no responsibility for publication of the work. A similar situation occurs when a commercial publisher arranges to publish the card catalog of a library in book form. The library has no real responsibility for publication; it has only given permission to the commercial publisher to undertake publication. However, since the content of the catalog has been prepared by the library's cataloging staff, the content of the publication originates with the library. In all those cases, consider that 'originates with' is equivalent to 'emanates from'."

Source: Library of Congress Rule Interpretations, Second Edition, 1989. Rule 21.1B2 "Applicability," p. 1.

the specific map. This concept is difficult to grasp at first for the cataloger who is used to working with monographs, but the rule itself, and, more important, the LC Rule Interpretation for 21.1B2(f), does provide the needed information to clarify this unique situation.

In fact, by carefully studying the Rule Interpretation for 21.1B2 one can gain a better understanding of the circumstances surrounding what constitutes an "emanating" agency and when that agency can be determined to be the main entry for the item. First, review Category F in the Rule Interpretation, which states:

> Use judgment in deciding whether the corporate body is the producer of the cartographic work, i.e., take into account such factors as the nature of the body and its cartographic output as well as any special information about the cartography of a particular work.

The more obvious examples of "the nature of the body and its cartographic output" include the U.S. Geological Survey and the individual state geological surveys in the United States, similar national and territorial geological surveys of other countries, longtime map-producing companies such as Rand McNally and the American Automobile Association, and scientific organizations such as the National Geographic Society. Similarly, in other countries, agencies, companies, and organizations are well-known for their cartographic output, e.g., the British Ordnance Survey and its earlier form of the Directorate of Overseas Surveys, the Institute Geographique National in France, Falk Verlag and Mairs Geographischer Verlag in Germany, and Geomatics Canada or the Geological Survey of Canada. Further, "special information about the cartography of a particular work" simply means that a corporate body has been formally stated as the body that did the cartographic work, using phrases such as "Cartography by . . ." and "Cartographically produced . . .".

Beyond the well-known companies or agencies that produce maps are many other lesser-known ones that either directly produce maps or indirectly "cause" them to be produced. The first page of the Rule Interpretation delineates three conditions in category "A," in which a corporate body caused the map to be created (see Box 8.1). The last condition states that "d) If there is doubt that the work emanates from the corporate body, assume that the corporate body is involved with the work," which doesn't help specify if this should then be considered the main entry but does seem to indicate that the corporate body involved should be traced at least as an added entry, for the possibility that it created the map or caused it to be created.

Many of the well-known cartographic agencies or companies mentioned typically fall into subcategory "a". These agencies or companies would be given main entry status unless an individual was formally named as the creator, or author if you will, of the map. See the later section "Terms that Indicate Responsibility for the Map" for helpful terms that formalize a statement of responsibility. The same is true with the other two categories—if an individual is named as the responsible party for the map, then he or she is given main entry status and any corporate bodies may be traced as an added entry unless they are strictly commercial publishers.

Category "b", where the first corporate body has caused the map to be issued, is fairly common with maps but often lacks explicit statements to guide the cataloger to an understanding of what has transpired between the two corporate bodies involved. Besides the example given, which shows an explicit relationship, there are examples of an implied situation where one corporate body has caused (has contracted with the second, publishing, corporate body to get the map published) another corporate body to issue the map. These may include local chambers of commerce or convention and visitors bureaus contracting with a commercial publisher (see Figure 8.1), sometimes a cartographic publisher and sometimes not, to produce a map of a city or community, and commercial banks working with a cartographic publisher or even a local chamber or bureau to produce a map showing the locations of their bank branches (see Figure 2.3 in Chapter 2).

Finally, in category "c", a typical situation is when a local government agency, such as a planning or zoning agency or department of engineering, controls the content of the map by way of holding the data involved, but a company publishes the map. The government agency is given as the main entry because the map "originates with" that agency.

COPYRIGHT HOLDERS AS RESPONSIBLE PARTIES

Yet another condition in which a corporate body may be determined as the main entry for a map is if the company or agency is the copyright holder. Normally the copyright holder might have a role as only publisher of an item (see the LC Rule Interpretation for Rule 1.4D1, second paragraph for one such case). If, however, no other statement of responsibility is named on the item, then it is presumed

OCLC: 33630270   Rec stat: c

Entered: 19951121   Replaced: 20010612   Used: 19960228

Type: e   ELvl: I   Srce: d   Relf: Ctrl: Lang: eng

BLvl: m   Form: GPub: SpFm: MRec: Ctry: cau

CrTp: a   Indx: 1   Proj: DtSt: s   Dates: 1995,

Desc: a

```
 1 040     UPM |c UPM |d OCL
 2 007     a |b j |d c |e a |f n |g z |h n
 3 034 1   a |b 34000
 4 034 0   a
 5 043     n-us-ca
 6 052     4364 |b L8:2V3
 7 052     4362 |b S216
 8 090     G4364.L8:2V3 1995 |b .M5
 9 090     |b
10 049     UPMM
11 110 2   Mid San Fernando Valley Chamber of Commerce.
12 245 10  Your map to the heart of the San Fernando Valley / |c Mid San
Fernando Valley Chamber of Commerce, Valley Chamber Services.
13 255     Scale [ca. 1:34,000].
14 255     Scale not given.
15 260     [Van Nuys, Calif.?] : |b sales & production co-ordination by Siena
Publishing, |c [1995?]
16 300     2 maps on 1 sheet : |b both sides, col. ; |c 39 x 47 cm. and 27 x 35
cm., sheet 55 x 87 cm., folded to 22 x 10 cm.
17 500     Panel title.
18 500     Includes street index, tourist information, community services direc-
tory, ill., and advertisements.
19 505 0   [Van Nuys metropolitan area] -- [San Fernando Valley].
20 651  0  Van Nuys (Los Angeles, Calif.) |v Maps.
21 651  0  San Fernando Valley (Calif.) |v Maps.
```

FIGURE 8.1. Chamber of Commerce Main Entry Record (*Source:* WorldCat Database, the OCLC Online Union Catalog [WorldCat], see <http://www.oclc. org/firstsearch/database/details/dbinformation_WorldCat.html>.)

that the corporate entity not only holds copyright but also was respon-sible for the creation of the map. This is particularly true for those corporate entities which are known to be cartographic publishers.

On rare occasions a person is shown to hold copyright to a map and also may have been formally named as being responsible for its cre-ation. For example, the map titled "Vermont Covered Bridges" (see

Figure 8.2) includes the formal statement of responsibility "sketches by C. Roy Moore" followed by the copyright symbol. In such cases, the person named is given in the statement of responsibility and as the main entry and understood also to have published the map.

In either case, the bottom line is that the corporate body or person who holds copyright to the map is considered likely to be responsible for the creation of the map if no other statement indicates responsibility.

TERMS THAT INDICATE RESPONSIBILITY FOR A MAP

Note the terms "mapped," "edited," and "produced" in the example used to show what "emanating" means in the earlier discussion. Such a statement on a map is indicative of responsibility for the map's creation. A list of terms such as these is found with the APPLICATION to

```
OCLC: 47624830        Rec stat:  n
Entered:  20010721    Replaced:  20010721    Used:  20010721
Type: e    ELvl: I   Srce: d    Relf:     Ctrl:      Lang: eng
BLvl: m    Form:     GPub:      SpFm:     MRec:      Ctry: vtu
CrTp: a    Indx: 0   Proj:      DtSt: s   Dates: 1946,
Desc: a
 1 040     UPM c UPM
 2 007     a |b j |d a |e a |f n |g z |h n
 3 034 0   a
 4 043     n-us-vt
 5 052     3751
 6 090     G3751.P24 1946 |b .M6
 7 090     |b
 8 049     UPMM
 9 100 1   Morse, C. Roy.
10 245 10 Vermont covered bridges |h [map] / |c sketches by C. Roy Morse
[copyright].
11 255     Scale not given.
12 260     [Vermont?] : |b C. Roy Morse, |c 1946.
```

FIGURE 8.2. Portion of Record Showing an Individual As Copyright Holder (*Source:* WorldCat Database, the OCLC Online Union Catalog [WorldCat], see <http://www.oclc.org/firstsearch/database/details/dbinformation_WorldCat.html>.)

Rule 1F1 in *Cartographic Materials*. These terms are extremely helpful in determining the presence of a statement of responsibility. The following is the full list as shown in *Cartographic Materials*. Also, any of these terms may be associated with either a personal name or a corporate body.

artwork
by
cartographer
cartography by
compiled *or* recompiled
corrected
created *or* recreated
dedicated by . . . to; *or,* dedicated to . . . by (*not* dedicated to . . .)
delineated
designed
done *or* redone
drafted *or* redrafted *(if it appears alone on the cartographic item)*
drawn
edited *or* re-edited
engraved *(if it appears alone on the cartographic item)*
made *or* remade
made up
prepared
produced
revised
reworked
surveyed
updated

Notice that this list includes not only the term "by," which is probably the most commonly used term in association with an author's name for a monograph, but also "compiled," "designed," and "edited or re-edited", among many others. Some of these terms would not be considered indicative of responsibility for a monograph except under very specific circumstances. In other words, due to the nature of a map, an individual's or corporate body's work related to the map's creation typically calls for a range of skills, responsibilities, and/or division of labor. Therefore, the labels used to convey responsibility are broader and more widely interpreted for maps than are those for authors of textual works.

"PROMINENCE" AND ITS RELATION TO STATEMENT OF RESPONSIBILITY

Although terms that indicate responsibility for a map are very helpful in deciding who or what should be given main entry status, the cataloger cannot make this choice unless the statement of responsibility appears "prominently" on the map. The concept of prominence is dealt with in Rule 1.1F1 in AACR2R: "Transcribe statements of responsibility appearing prominently in the item in the form in which they appear there." So, what exactly does "prominently" mean and/or entail? That is a fair question, and one that is not completely answered by Rule 0.8 in AACR2R, which states:

> The word *prominently* . . . means that a statement to which it applies must be a formal statement found in one of the prescribed sources of information . . . for areas 1 and 2 for the class of material to which the item being catalogued belongs.

Now, I'm not sure about you, the reader, but Rule 0.8 really isn't that enlightening to me! The easy part of that rule is the "found in one of the prescribed sources of information." As the APPLICATION to Rule 1F1 in *Cartographic Materials* reminds us, "For maps, charts, etc., the whole item is the chief source of information, therefore, if a statement of responsibility appears anywhere on the item, record it." Thus, we don't have to concern ourselves with the location of the information. What is still somewhat mysterious, and at the crux of Rule 0.8, is the "formal statement" mentioned in that passage. Neither AACR2R nor *Cartographic Materials* clarifies this phrase, so we must turn to *Merriam-Webster's Collegiate Dictionary* (http://www. m-w.com/home.htm) to discern what is meant by a "formal" statement in terms of statement of responsibility.

Webster's defines "formal" in three ways, the first of which may help us:

1 a : belonging to or constituting the form or essence of a thing <formal cause> **b** : relating to or involving the outward form, structure, relationships, or arrangement of elements rather than content <formal logic> <formal style of painting> <formal approach to comparative linguistics>

Part "b" touches on what we are after, relationships and the arrangement of elements. In our case, those elements are who or what has caused the map to be created. Therefore, a formal statement must be one that explicitly states which individual(s) or company(ies)/ agency(ies) played a role in the map's existence, and this returns us to looking for terms, such as those mentioned previously, that formalize such a statement. Terms such as "cartography by", "drafted" or "draughtsman", and even "drawn by" constitute identifying a formal relationship between person/agency and the map.

Two other elements assist in defining a "formal" statement when it comes to maps: (1) prominence in terms of layout, or location, of a person's or company's/agency's name in association with the title of the map and (2) a recognized logo or brand name of a cartographic-producing company, such as those for many federal agencies, e.g., the U.S. National Forest Service (see Figure 8.3), or a company such as the American Automobile Association (AAA). Either of these conditions, or a combination of both, meets the definition of prominence for map producers and therefore justifies naming them in the Statement of responsibility area and/or as the main entry in the bibliographic record.

The first condition, i.e., layout, may also mean a stylistic approach whereby the name may be bolded, italicized, or even printed using a different color to make it stand out, hence "prominence." The layout constitutes the "appearing prominently in the item in the form in which they appear" part of Rule 1.1F1. The first condition also means

FIGURE 8.3. U.S. National Forest Service Logo

that a person's or agency's/company's name is linked with the title by its position as a part of that title, e.g., the Stanford Map of Europe or Belden's Illustrated Atlas of the County of Victoria, Ontario, 1881. The name also may be near the title or physically part of the title area, most usually directly above or below the title itself. For example, maps produced by the U.S. National Forest Service typically present, just above the title of the map, "United States Department of Agriculture, National Forest Service." As you catalog maps from a larger variety of sources, the concepts of "formal" and "prominence" will become more apparent and easier to understand.

SUMMARY

1. If a formal statement of responsibility given on the map names a person(s) , or if a person's name appears as part of the title, or if a person's name indicates responsibility for the map by layout or typography, enter the map by the individual's name or by the first named person if no more than three persons are named. Provide added entries for other personal names if they appear as part of the statement of responsibility, up to two, or if they are named elsewhere as providing a contribution to the creation of the map.

2. Enter the map under a corporate body if authorship is not attributed to a person, following the stipulation in Rule 21.1B2(f) that the map must "emanate" from that corporate body. If the corporate body performs as only publisher of the map, then main entry must be under title. Again, if the corporate body is not named as part of a formal statement of responsibility in relation to using an indicative term but is prominently shown on the map by layout, typography, or the use of a logo or brand for the body itself, then enter the map by that named body. Rule 21.30E1 instructs us to make an added entry for any other corporate body that played a role in the creation of the map "unless it functions solely as distributor or manufacturer." In addition, "[m]ake an added entry under a prominently named publisher if the responsibility for the work extends beyond that of merely publishing the item being catalogued. In case of doubt, make an added entry."

3. Finally, enter the map under its title if no personal authorship is given and it does not emanate from a corporate body or if authorship is diffuse. Diffuse authorship means that four or more persons and/or

corporate bodies are given on the map and principal responsibility is not attributed to any of the first three authors given. In the case of diffuse authorship, Rule 21.6C2 indicates to "[m]ake an added entry under the heading for the first person or corporate body named."

Chapter 9

Providing a Title for the Record

Determining a title for the bibliographic record is not always straightforward when it comes to maps for two reasons. First, depending on the genre of map, there may be two or more titles to choose from and these may come from a variety of locations on the map and/or its container. Second, even if the map has only one title, that single title can be read in more than one way due to either the size and style of typography or the elements of the title being scattered, or both. This latter case is typically known as the "layout" of the title and requires close attention, unlike providing a title from the title page of a book. So, the cataloger's goal is to provide both a title for the 245 field and any number of additional titles, either due to their number or their readability, as additional access points in the record.

WHEN ONLY ONE TITLE EXISTS

If only one title is on the item, naturally, the cataloger must use it. Although this seems straightforward enough, be aware that, as mentioned previously, typography and/or layout may allow the cataloger to trace for this title in a different form. Second, at times, the resulting title simply is so vague as not to provide meaningful geographic access to the map. When this happens, the cataloger can add information to the title for clarity following Rule 3.1E1. This circumstance is further elucidated in a later section, Other Title Circumstances.

CHOOSING A TITLE WHEN THERE IS MORE THAN ONE

When there is more than one title to choose from, the primary concern is to *provide the most comprehensive title in terms of both geo-*

graphic area and topic. When only one title is present and its layout is straightforward, the task is made simple. However, the cataloger often must make a choice. Fortunately, *Cartographic Materials* and the LC *Map Cataloging Manual* (MCM) assist us with interpreting Rule 3.1B3 in AACR2R to its fullest extent. While the rule states to "choose the title proper on the basis of the sequence or layout of the titles" and "[i]f these are insufficient to enable the choice to be made or are ambiguous, choose the most comprehensive title" it doesn't tell us how to do this. Use the following outline, reordered from the table following Rule 1B86 in *Cartographic Materials,* as a step-by-step guide (see also Figure 9.1):

I. Steps in Choosing the Title
   A. Consider *all of the titles on the map* and pick the one that includes the most precise expression of *both* area and subject.
   B. Consider *all of the titles on the map* and pick the one that *includes the geographic area* and is in *the most preferred location* (see A-E under II for location).
   C. Pick the title in *the most preferred location* (see A-E under II for location).
II. Order of Preferred Location
   A. Title located *within the neat line or border* of the main map
   B. Title *from the recto but outside the neat line or border* of the main map
   C. *Panel title*
   D. Title *from the verso* of the cartographic item
   E. Title from the *cover, container, envelope, etc.*

PROVIDING FOR ADDITIONAL TITLES AND/OR DIFFERENT WAYS TO READ THE CHOSEN TITLE

Once the title proper has been chosen for use in the 245 field, we need also to provide access to additional titles found elsewhere on the map and its container, if appropriate. We also need to provide access

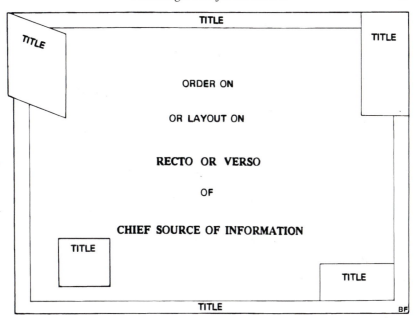

FIGURE 9.1. Choice of Title Proper in Cases of More Than One Title (*Source:* Reproduced from *Cartographic Materials: A Manual of Interpretation for the AACR2,* 1982, p. 25. Permission granted by the American Library Association.)

for those times when the title proper can be read differently due to its typography or layout.

When typography and/or layout play a role in how a single title can be interpreted by the reader, it is appropriate to trace for these alternative methods of reading the title. In the case of typography, the title may have been typeset using a color to make a word or set of words stand out or a word or set of words is capitalized compared to surrounding words in upper- and lowercase. This is usually done with those words which indicate geographic area to give them prominence in the title. Sometimes the script used with particular words causes them to stand out as well. The cataloger should also be attuned to abbreviations and the effect that they might have in terms of retrieval of a title in a citation list within a particular online public access catalog (OPAC). Place names in titles are frequently abbreviated as an example.

The other situation that comes to bear is commonly known as a "scattered title." Here, individual or sets of words from the title have been spaced so that their order can be read and understood in more than one way; *or* they may be placed on the sheet physically separated by a significant distance, such as in the top-left and top-right corners of the map sheet; *or* they may be separated physically by sheets of paper, such as when a single map is produced on multiple sheets and the entire title can be read only when those sheets are laid side by side. To make things even more complicated, both typography and layout can be jointly used in a publication, such as in the National Geographic "Topo map" or "Destination map" series.

In the case of additional titles from different locations, *it is not necessary to trace these separately if the wording is identical to the chosen title proper.* For those not falling under the circumstance of identical wording, trace the titles in a 246 field using the means of providing a leading phrase to identify the origin of the additional titles. For instance:

245   10 State College, Pa. and its surrounding area
246   1 $i Panel title: $a Welcome to State College, Pennsylvania and the Pennsylvania State University

No matter the circumstance, once the primary title has been chosen for the bibliographic record, the cataloger should also be ready to provide additional titles that make sense in terms of readability, clarity, and access. A helpful chart of 246 field circumstances that includes the correct indicator values is shown in Table 9.1. This is also found in electronic form at <http://www.libraries.psu.edu/iasweb/catsweb/tools/catref.htm>.

THE "SCATTERED TITLE" PHENOMENON
AND HOW TO HANDLE IT

I mentioned earlier a situation known as "scattered title" that sometimes occurs with the production of a map and noted that this can occur all on the same sheet or across multiple sheets making up a single map. Our map cataloging "bible," *Cartographic Materials,* provides an understandable decision table (located with the APPLICA-

TABLE 9.1. 246 Field Cheat Sheet Quick Reference Guide

Most Commonly Used Varying Titles

246	14	Cover title
246	18	Spine title
246	1	$i Phrase: $a Title
246	3	And/&, i.e., [sic], spelled out number, collective title, abbreviations*
246	30	Portions of title (parts of 245)
246	31	Parallel title

	Indicator Values		
Type of Varying Title	**Ind. 1**	**Ind. 2**	**Form of Note**
Added title page title	1	5	Title
*Alternate form of word in 245 title	3		Title
Alternative 245 title due to layout	3	0	Title
At head of title	1		$i At head of title: $a Title
Binder's title	1		$i Binder's title: $a Title
Caption title	1	6	Title
Colophon title	1		$i Title from colophon: $a Title
Corrected form of title (sic. or i.e.)	3		Title
Cover title	1	4	Title
Half title	1		$i Half title: $a Title
Incorrect form of title ([sic] in 245)	3		Title
No collective title (access via a character string consisting of all titles immediately adjacent to one another and appearing at the beginning of the 245)	3		Title
No added entry for varying title	0		$i Introductory phrase: $a Title
Other title info. from 245	3	0	Title
Other title info. *not* from 245; source supplied by cataloger in $i	1		$i Introductory phrase: $a Title
Parallel title from 245	3	1	Title

TABLE 9.1 *(continued)*

Parallel title from cover	1	4	Title
Parallel title from added title page	1	5	Title
Parallel title from spine	1	8	Title
Parallel title from source supplied by cataloger in $i	1		$i Introductory phrase: $a Title
Part/Section title from 245	3	0	Title
Portion of title proper that is emphasized by typography or other similar conditions	3	0	Title
Portion of title proper without introductory terms	3	0	Title
Running title	1	7	Title
Spine title	1	8	Title
Title on container	1		$i Title on container: $a Title
Vols. [no.]-[no.] have title:		1	$i Vols. [no.]-[no.] have title: $a Title
Any other condition not covered by one of the above categories	1		$i Introductory phrase: $a Title

Source: Adapted from Library of Congress, Washington, DC, *Cataloging Service Bulletin: Collections Services,* No. 68, Spring 1975, pp. 3-4.

TION following Rule 1B8b) when the cataloger has to create the primary title from scattered title elements. As noted at the beginning of the table, "[i]f the area and subject of the cartographic item do not occur together as a single title, but are 'scattered' over the item, construct a title in natural reading order, based on the following order of preference":

1. Any element that is *distinguished by typography and/or position*
2. Any element that *includes the format (e.g., map)* and the preposition "of"
3. Any element that *includes the area*
4. Any element that *includes the subject*

5. Any element that *includes the scale information* and that is in a position which suggests inclusion in the title
6. Any element that *includes the date* and is in a position which suggests inclusion in the title

To clarify, "typography" means size and/or color of lettering used, the script or font chosen for one or more words to make them more pronounced, and even the use of bolding, italics, and underlining or a combination of any of these to bring attention to a word or set of words in the title. "Position" means both where the words are located on the item and possibly their proximity to other words and the direction that a word or set of words runs, for instance from bottom to top as opposed to left to right. By putting the scattered words together in a readable format, the cataloger can successfully provide a single title that is meaningful both geographically and topically.

WHEN TO USE A COLLECTIVE TITLE AS PRIMARY TITLE

If a single sheet includes multiple main maps, otherwise known as "component maps," none of which can be considered primary or more important than the others, but each of which has its own title, and whenever a map series contains sheets in which each of them has an individual title but also a title that appears on all sheets, a title is given that provides an overarching, or "collective," title for all of the maps involved. Rule 1.1B10 in AACR2R outlines what to do in this particular situation: "If the chief source of information bears both a collective title and the titles of individual works, give the collective title as the title proper and give the titles of the individual works in a contents note." An option to providing the component map titles in only a contents note, if they are few in number and access to them is important, is to provide each of them in its own 246 Varying Form of Title field, using the "Other title information not from 245" category.

In the former circumstance, a map panel or cover often provides a collective title that is inclusive of all of the component maps involved. In the latter case, a collective title must appear on each of the sheets in the set or series for it to be "collective"; often this type of collective title includes the scale of the geographic area covered by the set. In other instances, a collective title may come from a container, such as an envelope. In all of these cases make sure to provide a "Source of title" note, such as "Title from envelope" or "Panel title," so that users of the bibliographic record are aware of the circumstances involved. Sometimes a map series lacks a unifying title for the series, leaving a situation in which the cataloger must provide a collective title (see the following section for guidance in this case).

WHAT TO DO WITH AN UNTITLED MAP

What do we do if there is no title on the map or its container to use? Rule 3.1B4 tells us to construct a title for the item and to "[a]lways include in the supplied title the name of the area covered." This is of extreme importance with maps, but one must also attempt to be succinct yet clear in supplying the name of the geographic area. Make sure that the title is enclosed in square brackets. Last, in this particular circumstance, make sure to provide a general note stating that the title has been supplied by the cataloger; most usually this is worded "Title supplied by cataloger."

OTHER TITLE CIRCUMSTANCES

Naturally, if a map has parallel titles and other title information available, this information needs to be recorded. Follow the rules in AACR2R to accomplish this last step. Pay close attention to Rule 3.1E2, though, which covers the circumstance of when the resulting choice of title lacks a clear indication of geographic area. This is when the cataloger can supply just the other title information, in the form of geographic area covered by the map. Again, one should enclose the provided information in square brackets in these cases to further assist library patrons who are searching for maps by geographic area.

PROVIDING A "SOURCE OF TITLE" NOTE

Although the following is covered in Chapter 14, which details the types and order of notes that should be given in the record, I want to discuss the "Source of Title" note here, as this follows directly from the circumstances of needing to choose between two or more titles and having to construct a title. Although this might not be important to library patrons, it can be very helpful to other catalogers attempting to identify matching copy from a bibliographic utility.

A common practice is to provide a "Source of Title" note whenever the chosen title comes from a location *other than from within the map's neat line or the map itself.* The most common locations are called the "panel" and the "cover," and the corresponding notes given read simply "Panel title" and "Cover title," with earlier variations being "Title from panel" and "Title from cover." The circumstances regarding when to choose the panel title or cover title over the title with the map itself were outlined earlier in the order of preferred locations, but to further elucidate, if the title with the map or within the neat line of the map gives only the geographic area or only the topic involved, but the panel or cover title gives both, choose the panel or cover title for use as the title proper.

Panel Title versus Cover Title

It is important to understand the difference between "panel" and "cover" in terms of the physical map and to be able to distinguish between the two, both for giving an accurate "Source of title" note and for the purpose of giving a complete set of dimensions in the Physical Description field.

A "panel" is a comprehensive part of the physical sheet on which the map is printed; i.e., when the map sheet is laid flat, the panel is a part of that same sheet of paper. In addition, when the map is folded, the panel is intended to be the part of the sheet that displays itself to the user before the user opens the sheet to see the map inside.

On the other hand, a "cover" is just that, an outer cover into which the map sheet is folded, and although it usually is physically attached to the map sheet, it doesn't necessarily have to be. The cover can be unattached or removed (if you are careful in the process!) and it does not affect the physical map sheet itself; just the opposite would be true for a panel title area (you would literally have to take a pair of scissors and cut the panel area from the sheet in order to remove the panel title). Most usually the cover is made of a heavier paper or card stock and may be laminated with an outer clear coating for further protection and/or eye appeal.

In both cases the title that appears usually differs from the title found on the map. It is the author's experience that the title found on the panel for city maps typically is more comprehensive, i.e., provides both geographic area and topic, than that found with the map itself and therefore is the better choice for the title proper in the bibliographic record. When choosing to use the panel or cover title, then, the "Source of Title" note is to be employed, and just as important, the title found with the map itself is to be entered in a 246 field.

Finally, since the Chief source of information for cartographic materials provides for the use of titles from containers such as envelopes or map tubes, also provide appropriate information in this note as to the origin of the main title, such as "Title from envelope," if the circumstance called for using a title from this source.

Chapter 10

Edition

Naturally, maps can be produced in editions, just as other kinds of materials may be. The revision of even a small portion of the cartographic information has a significant impact on the meaning of the information shown. This relates, again, to the fact that maps convey their meaning, intent, and information primarily in a graphic form as opposed to textual. Therefore, even small changes magnify the difference in information provided to the user with each new edition. Thus, statements of revision are considered extremely important with maps.

Rule 3.2B1 states that we need to "[t]ranscribe a statement relating to an edition of a work that contains differences from other editions of that work, or to a named reissue of a work, as instructed in 1.2B." When providing an edition statement, words such as "edition" and "revised" or "revision" may be abbreviated and numbers in textual form may be changed to their numerical form as allowed for in Rule 1.2B1 in AACR2R. In addition, Rule 3.2E in AACR2R says to "[t]ranscribe a statement of responsibility relating to one or more named revisions of an edition . . . as instructed in 1.2E and 3.1F." (See the last example in the following list for formatting an edition statement with a named statement of responsibility.) Examples of some typical cartographic edition statements include the following:

Ed. 2-GSGS.
1`ere éd. 1980. (on map: 1`ere édition: 1980)
Rev. 1995. (on map: Revised 1995)
Provisional ed.
Photorevised 1974.
1st ed. 1965. (on map: Primera edici'on 1965)
New ed. (on map panel: New edition!)
Rev. and updated 1990. (on map: Logging information revised and updated in 1990)
Rev. Sept. 1992. (on map: Revised September 1992)
Rev. Feb. 1973 / |b K.A.M. (on map: Revised Feb. 1973 K.A.M.)

Also, the "Optional addition" of Rule 3.2B3 allows the cataloger to supply an edition statement in square brackets if the map involved is known to contain significant changes from a previous edition of the same map but lacks an edition/revision statement. This is most easily determined by comparing the earlier edition of the map to the one being cataloged and noticing changes to any part of the cartographic content.

EDITIONS TO INDIVIDUAL SHEETS IN A MAP SERIES

Map series can also be produced in editions, including what are known as preliminary editions. That is, each of the individual maps in the series may be produced at the same time or over a range of time, but from the same cartographic agency. It is not uncommon, however, in a given map collection to find that specific sheets are from different editions. This may occur either because the map collection involved was intended to provide complete geographic coverage for an area, such as a country, at a given scale, or in terms of the publication cycle, it may be due to such vagaries as geographic coverage never being completed for a specific scale within one edition. Sheets of different editions may also be put together to complete a set or series when map collections include incomplete map sets or series given as gifts; the individual sheets from the differing editions help complete the coverage needed. In any of these cases, the edition statement "Various ed." should be given in square brackets, followed by a general note specifying which editions are involved and how many sheets are included from each edition, if this is easy to determine.

UNCERTAINTY REGARDING AN EDITION STATEMENT

Sometimes a statement on a map may lead the cataloger to believe that a particular edition is involved, but doubt exists because a clear word such as "edition" is not part of that statement. Rule 1.2B3 in AACR2R assists us somewhat by identifying three words that do indicate a particular edition of a work: *edition, issue,* and *version,* or their equivalents in other languages. Take care not to confuse statements regarding printings or reissues of a map with edition statements. Also, if a formal edition statement is present and another statement seemingly concerns the edition, such as "Second Edition: U.T.M. grid added by D.O.S. 1966 . . . ," then add such a statement as a quoted note, since the formal edition statement takes precedence. If enough doubt exists regarding any possible edition statement, it is best to exercise cataloger's judgment and give it as a full or partial quoted note instead of as an edition statement.

Finally, the cataloger should follow the rules in AACR2R outlining a couple of other circumstances relating to editions, such as statements of responsibility relating to subsequent edition statements and items lacking a collective title but being described as a unit where multiple editions are present (see Rule 3.2B5 in AACR2R).

Chapter 11

Mathematical Data Area

This area causes the most consternation and suffering for those new to creating bibliographic records for maps. Although the three primary parts of information housed in this field are scale, projection, and coordinates, other mathematical data can also be placed here. This additional mathematical data would be for maps of the heavens that contain information about declination and zenith. But in the vast majority of cases, scale, projection, and coordinates will adequately fill this space in the bibliographic record.

Although this is the most technical part of working with maps, as noted at the beginning of this book, with time and constant exposure, the cataloger will find this area much less mysterious and difficult. Perhaps it would be a good idea to go back to Chapter 1, "Background" to review what Drazniowsky and others said about the special aspects of maps in terms of displaying three-dimensional reality on a two-dimensional sheet of paper. This transfer requires scale and projection. Coordinates are the way-finding mechanism for identifying a particular location, both in real life and on paper. Without these mathematical machinations, reality could never be portrayed accurately and our comprehension of both place and location would be severely limited.

The other problematic part of dealing with the 255 and 034 fields and the information placed within them is that it takes time to learn the correct way to display the information. Punctuation and spacing, and in particular the diacritics used with coordinates, have specific meanings and/or assist in readability and understanding the information. Again, practice and time will make this aspect of map cataloging much more palatable. We must provide this information accurately so that library patrons can use this information to decide whether to pursue the actual map, according to their needs.

SCALE INFORMATION

Scale is given on a map in a multiplicity of ways, or not at all! This includes simply describing the scale with words or a mixture of words and numbers, commonly known as a "verbal scale"; showing it as a mathematical formula, which is known as a "representative fraction" (RF); or using some form of segmented line, known as a "bar scale" or "graphic scale." One may find that a combination of these is sometimes also employed in the creation of a map. For a graphic example of the variety of methods used to show scale, see Figure 11.8 at the end of this chapter. In addition, the scale can be given as being the accurate scale, such as "1:24,000" or "one inch equals eight miles," or as an approximation, usually by using the word "approximately" or one of its abbreviations, "ca." or "approx." Also, sometimes, the use of such words as "nearly" or "about" also indicates an approximate scale in a verbal scale statement. Knowing the difference between exact and approximate scales is important in terms of employing "ca." and/or square brackets correctly in the scale statement.

Note that a "scale statement" may include no scale given on the map in any form, the simplest of all situations. Other situations include a map that explicitly states that the map was not drawn according to any scale; a map in which the scale varies from the center of the map outward; having multiple maps on one sheet, each with its own scale or a combination of no scale and specific scales; and having multiple maps on separate sheets, each with its own scale, with a consistent scale for all of the maps, or a combination of no scale and different scales. Let's examine each situation relating to scale, going from the simplest to the most complex. We'll begin the discussion by focusing on cataloging a single map without a scale given or with one scale and move on to multiple scales for multiple maps under the topic of "Scales differ," roughly following the order of rules in Chapter 3 under 3.3B.

Before we can begin, however, Rule 3.3B1 says that we must provide a scale statement for each map that we catalog, and that if a scale is given, it must be in the form of a representative fraction, i.e., 1:xx,xxx. Just as important, with the singular exception of "Not drawn to scale," the scale statement always starts with the word *Scale* or *Scales,* as the case may be, as delineated in this same rule. Therefore, the "scale statement" is a combination of the word "Scale(s)" and the representative fraction that follows it, e.g., Scale [ca. 1:175,000], or the word "Scale" followed by the rest of a worded statement, as noted in the following section.

No Scale Is Given or the Map Is Not Drawn to Scale

The simplest situation occurs when scale is not given in any form on the map or maps involved. In such situations, give the statement "Scale not given" in 255 subfield "a" and move on to the projection and coordinate areas. Be aware, however, that if a scale statement appears as part of the title, this *does* constitute a scale statement, even if it does not occur anywhere else on the map, and you then would give the scale in the 255 subfield "a" in its RF form.

Another easy situation occurs when the map has a statement that specifies that the map is not drawn to any scale at all, usually in the form of "This map is not drawn to scale" or something similar. This is not a common occurrence, but, for example, *National Geographic Magazine* often includes illustrative perspective maps that employ just such a phrase. Rule 3.3B5 in AACR2R addresses this particular situation. When such a situation as just described is encountered, therefore, use the standard phrase "Not drawn to scale."

Scale Statement Is Given As an Exact Scale

If the scale statement appears on the map or other prescribed source of information for this area, including as part of the title, whether in the form of a verbal scale or representative fraction, provide the scale as given. For example:

Item says: Scale 1:100,000
Record as: 255 Scale 1:100,000.

In a case where the scale, in RF form, is given only as part of the title, it is recorded in the same way, even if the scale does not appear elsewhere on the map. For example, if the title says "France, 1:50,000" or, more commonly, is given in one of the European forms of "1:50 000", "1:50.000", or "1:50/000", with the comma substituted by another type of punctuation or a space, and no other scale statement or graphic scale appears on the item, then the scale is given as "Scale 1:50,000" in the 255 field.

Remember that a scale given in its verbal form must be translated into the RF form according to Rule 3.3B1.

> *Item says:* One inch equals four miles *or* One inch = four miles
> *or* 1 inch to 4 miles *or* 1 inch = 4 miles *or* any of
> these with the words "inch" and/or "miles" abbreviated
> *Record as:* 255   Scale [1:253,440].

With the verbal scale, the RF must be placed in square brackets because the cataloger supplied the form of the scale as a representative fraction by converting the verbal terms into mathematical ones. Also, as noted earlier, even if the verbal scale appears only as part of the title, e.g., France at one to fifty thousand scale, and not given in a scale statement, record it as per the previous example, using square brackets.

Scale Statement Is Given As a Stated Approximation or Determined by the Cataloger

If the scale statement is given, in whichever form, as an approximate scale, then the use of the abbreviation "ca.", with or without square brackets, comes into play. Once again, the scale itself must be denoted in its RF form.

When the scale statement given on the map is either an RF or a verbal statement that includes the word "approximate" or "approximately" or one of its abbreviations, the RF must be given in the 255 subfield "a" with the abbreviation "ca."

> *Item says:* Scale ca. 1:24,000
> *Record as:* 255   Scale ca. 1:24,000.
> *Item says:* Scale equals approximately one inch to 4 miles
> *Record as:* 255   Scale [ca. 1:253,440].

The difference in the use of square brackets in this set of examples relates to the need for the cataloger to convert the verbal statement into the RF in the latter case.

Bar Scale, or Graphic Scale, Converted to a Representative Fraction

One of the most common forms of representing scale on a map is by the use of a bar, or graphic, scale. Although one may take a measurement along the graphic scale using a standard ruler and then convert the finding, e.g., measuring the length of a graphic scale that reads zero to one and then determining that one inch equals approximately one mile or approximately so many feet, which can then be calculated into one mile (see Figure 11.1 for two examples), the ingenious Natural Scale Indicator, mentioned in Chapter 3 in the Essential tools Available Only in Hard-Copy Form section, makes this chore unnecessary. By employing the Natural Scale Indicator correctly, first, by choosing the correct type of distance to be measured (e.g., using the mile graph for graphic scales measured in miles), then placing the "base line" of the Indicator on the zero mark of the graphic scale, and finally by reading where the one-mile mark lands on the Indicator, an approximate scale is easy to determine. The last illustration in Figure 11.1 shows a portion of the Natural Scale Indicator and demonstrates how to read it. I strongly encourage every map cataloger to purchase or find one of these handy tools to do your scale work as efficiently as possible.

The section of Rule 3.3B1 that says "[i]f no scale statement is found in the chief source of information or accompanying material nor on the item's container or case, estimate a representative fraction from a bar scale, or a grid. Give in square brackets the representative fraction preceded by ca." covers the aforementioned use of the Natural Scale Indicator.

Record as: 255   Scale [ca. 1:250,000].

Again, whenever the cataloger intervenes by creating a representative fraction, whether by doing a mathematical calculation based on a verbal statement or by reading an approximation from the Natural Scale Indicator, the RF must be given in square brackets.

"Scale Varies" and Its Correct Use

A very common error occurs when a cataloger gives the scale statement as "Scale varies" when he or she really has an item with

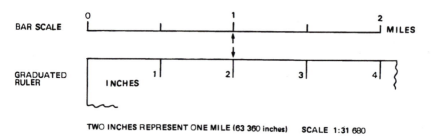

TWO INCHES REPRESENT ONE MILE (63 360 inches)   SCALE 1:31 680

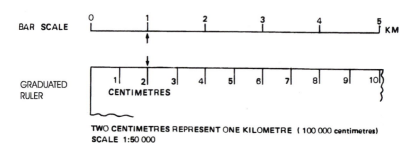

TWO CENTIMETRES REPRESENT ONE KILOMETRE (100 000 centimetres)
SCALE 1:50 000

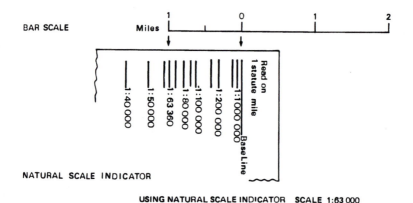

USING NATURAL SCALE INDICATOR   SCALE 1:63 000

FIGURE 11.1. Guidelines to Determine the Scale of a Map (*Source:* Reproduced from *Cartographic Materials: A Manual of Interpretation for the AACR2,* 1982, p. 168. Permission granted by the American Library Association.)

multiple scales, each of which is different. The "Scale varies" situation is very unusual, and cartographers create maps under this circumstance only for the explicit benefit of showing the geographic information at the center of the map at a larger scale (in other words, in more detail) than that at the outer margins of the geographic area. In such a case, the scale changes at a continuous ratio or at intervals on the map.

Provide the scale statement "Scale varies" *only* when the scale changes from the center of the map going outward toward the edges or border of the map *and the range of scales is not given* on the map itself. In addition, this statement applies to only one map on a sheet, not when different scales are used for two or more maps. This situation is covered in Rule 3.3B3 in AACR2R and is much more explicitly and clearly explained in the APPLICATION to Rule 3B3 and by way of a very clear illustration in *Cartographic Materials* (see Figure 11.2).

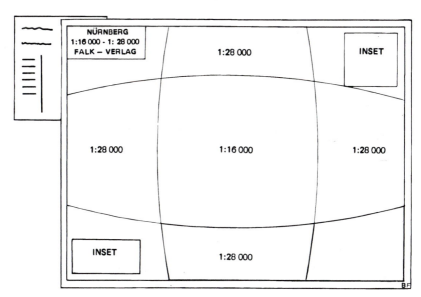

Scale changes at a continuous ratio, or at set intervals, out from centre
Scale 1:16 000–1:28 000

FIGURE 11.2. A "Scale Varies" Statement on a Single Map (*Source:* Reproduced from *Cartographic Materials: A Manual of Interpretation for the AACR2,* 1982, p. 54. Permission granted by the American Library Association.)

In those cases where "Scale varies" applies and the range of scales is given on the map, provide this information in the 034 and 255 fields in the following manner:

```
034 3   a |b 15000 |b 25000
255     Scale 1:15,000 -- 1:25,000.
```

Note that this is one of two instances in which multiple scales are given in both the 034 and 255 fields. A discussion of the options relating to multiple maps with different scales and providing multiple scales for them in the record follows.

Using "Scales Differ" Correctly and New Rule Changes Involved

What should you do if multiple maps are on one sheet or on more than one sheet and two or more scales are involved? Under the current rules, the cataloger would give separate scale statements if only two maps are involved, but if three or more maps are involved, the statement "Scales differ" would be given in a single 255 field. Rule 3.3B4 in AACR2R (1999 edition) discusses the former situation: "If the description is of a multipart item with two scales, give both. Give the larger scale first." Thus, there would be two 255 fields in the record, one for each scale, and, naturally, two matching 034 fields. However, note the phrase "multipart item" in the rule. What this does not take into account are those situations involving two maps on one sheet. The APPLICATION to Rule 3B4 in *Cartographic Materials,* and in addition, Rule 3B6, goes on to explain when to use the phrase "Scales differ" in terms of what are known as maps in components, or two maps on one sheet (which can be both maps on one side of the sheet or one map on each side of the sheet).

Rule 3.3B5 in AACR2R (1998 edition) provides for the latter situation: "If the description is of a multipart item with three or more scales, give *Scales vary.*" (Do not use "Scales vary" in this circumstance. The 2002 edition of AACR2R finally corrects this error by stating one should use the phrase *Not drawn to scale.*) However, once again, a rule, Rule 3B5, and its APPLICATION in *Cartographic Materials* not only more clearly outlines what to do with three or more maps, either in the case of a multipart item or maps in components, but also specifies using the correct phrase, "Scales differ."

Very recent changes to this area of the rules in the AACR2R were approved by the Joint Steering Committee for the Revision of Anglo-American Cataloging Rules (JSC) in late 2001 and should go into effect shortly before this book is published. The changes to the Mathematical Data Area (which will be renamed the Mathematical and Other Material Specific Details Area) regarding how to apply the current "rule of three" situation not only are different but also will allow catalogers the flexibility to make choices that either might work better in their particular situations or simply be more clear to users of the bibliographic records. Because of the departure from the current set of rules for multipart maps or component maps that are two or more in number, it is necessary to provide these changes in this book.

A New Method for Supplying Multiple Scales in the Bibliographic Record

As mentioned earlier, under the current rules, whenever two different scales are involved with multiple maps, each scale is given in its own scale statement; i.e., the record contains two 255 fields and, naturally, two 034 fields as well. Then, if three or more different scales are involved with multiple maps, the scale statement "Scales differ" is used in a single 255 field.

However, the changes in this Area of Chapter 3 provide the cataloger with other choices, based less on the number of differing scales and more on the circumstances of the same or different geographic areas involved. Most of the changes, as described here, have to do with relaxing the strict "rule of two" that has been in operation for many years and allowing the cataloger either to continue using "Scales differ" for two or more scales (here is the first change) or to provide as many scale statements as he or she deems necessary or appropriate to describe the maps accurately.

To be more precise, new *Options* to Rule 3.3B4 establish two circumstances in which multiple scales of two or more in number may be given, and in the second case, yet another option allows the cataloger to give multiple scales in different scale statements instead of a single statement, just as in the first circumstance, but paying attention to matching projection and/or coordinate information with the correct scale. These two circumstances are as follows:

a) If the description is of a cartographic item with two or more scales, when projection and/or coordinates are also different for each main item, give each scale in a separate scale statement. If there is more than one title, give the scale statements in the same order in which the titles are given. If there is only a collective title, give the largest scale first.

Scale 1:50,000 (W 94°42′04″—W 93°00′00″/N 49°00′00″—N 48°31′00″).

Scale 1:250,000 (W 94°43′—W 92°00′/N 49°00′—N 48°13′)

b) If the description is of a cartographic item with two or more scales, when projection and coordinates are the same for each main item, give the scales in one scale statement. If there is more than one title, give the scales in the same order in which the titles are given. If there is only a collective title, give the largest scale first.

Scale 1:7,819,000 and [ca. 1:15,000,000] (E 66°—E 138°/N 54°—N 18°)

Optionally, give each scale with its associated mathematical data in separate scale statements.

Scale 1:7,819,000 (E 66°—E 138°/N 54°—N 18°). – Scale [ca. 1:15,000,000] (E 66°—E 138°/N 54⁰—N 18°)

Let's examine each of these more closely. If the multiple maps involved are of different geographic areas, hence the "when projection and/or coordinates are also different for each main item" part of the rule, then give two or more separate scale statements. For instance, if maps of Pittsburgh and Allegheny County, Pennsylvania, are on the same sheet, obviously they would be at different scales, with the city map at a larger scale than the county map. Also, obviously, their coordinates would differ, while the projection used for each may or may not differ. In this case, give the scale and its related projection and/or coordinate information, if available, for Pittsburgh in the first 255 field, and the scale and related projection and/or coordinate information, if available, for Allegheny County in a second, separate 255 field. The order of the scale statements may be switched if, in the case of a noncollective title, the county map is given first and the city map is given second. Finally, if there is a single collective title, then the largest scale is given first; in this case it would again be the one for the city map.

In the second circumstance the multiple maps involved *are all for the same geographic area.* For instance, four maps of the United States may be on a single sheet or on multiple sheets, each map or sheet covering a different meteorological topic, such as average annual rainfall, average annual high and low temperatures, and average annual snowfall amounts. Since all of the maps involved are for the same area, in this case the United States, then the differing scale statements may be given in a single 255 field, along with their accompanying mathematical data, if available. This, in effect, is a summarization of the mathematical information because only one set of projections and/or coordinates would be given in one field. Again, the order of the maps given in the title or the collective title circumstances guides the order in which the scale statements are given.

Finally, the cataloger may choose the *Optional* route of the second circumstance and list each scale statement, with accompanying projection and/or coordinate information, in its own 255 field, no matter the number of scales involved. This option is a major departure from the "old" practice, whereby only two scales involved meant each was given in its own separate scale statement, but the use of three or more scales invoked the "Scales differ" phrase. However, map catalogers may continue to employ the former "rule of two" practice if they choose and ignore these changes altogether.

"Large Scale" versus "Small Scale": Uncovering the Mystery

The phrases "large scale" and "small scale" are used frequently by individuals in discussing the "size" of maps that they have in hand or are looking for in a collection. What is meant by these two terms and why are they difficult to understand?

The reason they are difficult to understand is that the words "large" and "small" do *not* refer to the size of the denominator in the representative fraction (see Figure 11.3). For example, a city map at a scale of 1:14,000 is considered a large-scale map, while a map of the country of Canada at a scale of 1:25,000,000 is considered a small-scale

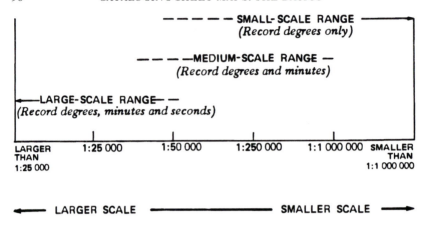

FIGURE 11.3. Map Scale Ranges for Recording Coordinates (*Source:* Reproduced from *Cartographic Materials: A Manual of Interpretation for the AACR2*, 1982, p. 58. Permission granted by the American Library Association.)

map. Note the anomaly of the large-scale number being 14,000 while the small scale number is 25,000,000—just the opposite of what our brains would expect to see!

In fact, the "large" and "small" designations refer to the level of detail that is available to include on a map when it is being made, and in the final product, then, by what can be seen by the map's user. Therefore, it is the scale that determines what and how much detail can be included. Large-scale maps show much detail in a small geographic area. The opposite is true for a small-scale map, which shows less detail but a much larger geographic area. For instance, most city maps are created at a large-scale range of somewhere between 1:10,000 and 1:40,000 depending on the size of the city or town being mapped. Maps at a scale of between approximately 1:75,000 and 1:200,000 usually are of good-sized regions or of many individual states in the United States, while much smaller scales on the order of 1:1,000,000 or higher are used to map countries and continents. World maps typically are at a scale of 1:25,000,000 or smaller.

To summarize, large-scale maps show "large" amounts of detail in a smaller geographic entity or area, such as a city, while small-scale maps show little or no detail, e.g., in terms of road networks and lacking all but the larger cities, but do cover a large geographic area. The U.S. Geological Survey's publication "Map Scale Fact Sheet 038-00

(April 2000)," available online at <http://mac.usgs.gov/mac/isb/pubs/factsheets/fs01502.html>, provides an excellent and easily understood discussion of map scale and its functionality, including a table of some of their products arranged by scale.

Additional Scale Information

Sometimes additional scale information, in the form of a verbal statement, may be given as part of the overall scale statement on the map. No doubt most catalogers are familiar with maps produced by the National Geographic Society, and in a majority of cases the Society will give additional scale information. A common feature is the scale statement in its representative fraction form followed by "or . . ." and its equivalent in verbal form. Such is the case with the October 1998 National Geographic map of Spain and Portugal, with the scale given as "Scale 1:2,074,000 or 1 inch = 33 miles." Similar in nature but different in form, other scale information may be given simply by listing the different forms after the scale in RF form without the preposition "or," e.g., "Scale 1:250,272. 1 in. equals 3.95 miles." In either case, the cataloger can give this information in the record, although it is optional to do so. However, if additional scale information is given, conclude the scale statement with a period, then proceed with giving the additional scale information, abbreviating such words as "inch," "centimeter," and "kilometer," but not "mile" or "miles." For example:

255   Scale 1:3,104,640. 1 in. = 49 miles.
255   Scale 1:450,000. At the equator.

What to Do When the Given Scale Is in Error

Every once in awhile an erroneous scale statement is given on a map. How should this be recorded in the bibliographic record? Naturally, we want to give the accurate scale for the item, but we also want to be explicit regarding the situation of the given scale being in error. In such a case, provide the accurate scale in square brackets, and naturally in its RF form, and follow that with a verbal statement in quotes, such as "not '1 in. equals 2 miles'," to explicitly give the information found on the map. For example, if you have a detailed city map with an exact scale given as "1:75,000" it is apparent that an extra zero was added erroneously to the scale statement, which should have been "1:7,500." The scale should be given as:

Scale [1:7,500] not "1:75,000".

Applying Vertical Scale

Certain types of sheet maps, as well as three-dimensional carto-graphic models, use what is known as vertical scale, in other words, providing a real-life dimension to a paper/model ratio of vertical distance. Rule 3.3B7 in AACR2R specifies where to place the vertical scale in the scale statement if a vertical scale is given. Naturally, if a vertical scale is not given in the Prescribed source of information, then this can be ignored, but for maps known as block diagrams or geologic profiles, vertical scale often is given and therefore needs to be a part of the bibliographic description.

So, when a vertical scale is given on the item, it is also given in the 255 field, following immediately after the horizontal scale and beginning with the phrase "Vertical scale" or "Vertical exaggeration," with the two scale statements separated by a period and space. The examples given with the rule are:

Scale 1:744,080. 1 in. to ca. 28 miles. Vertical scale ca. 1:96,000
Scale 1:250,000. Vertical exaggeration 1:5

What is the impact of a vertical scale on the 034 field? Whenever a vertical scale is given in the 255 field, then the Indicator value in the 034 field is set to "1" and a subfield "c" containing the denominator value of the vertical scale is given (see Figure 11.4).

The Power of "63360"

Do you know what 63360 represents? It is a powerful bit of infor-mation that you can use with a verbal or stated scale to help you quickly determine a representative fraction when you don't have a calculator handy, or even if you do! The number 63360 is how many inches are in one mile. Using this knowledge, if a map has a stated scale of "1 in. = 4 miles" simply multiply 63360 by 4 and you quickly

034 0 a
255   Scale not given.

034 0 a
255   Not drawn to scale.

034 0 a
255   Scale varies.

034 0 a
255   Scales differ.

034 0 a
255   Scale indeterminable.

034 1 a |b 55000
255   Scale [ca. 1:55,000].

- Do *not* use a comma in the 034 subfield "b" for the scale statement.
- When field 255 ends with a square bracket, it is acceptable to add a period to complete the line even though this creates a "double punctuation" situation, which is acceptable in only a few places elsewhere in the record.

034 1 a |b 1000000 |d W1250000 |e W0650000 |f N0500000 |g N0250000
255   Scale 1:1,000,000 |c (W 125°--W 65°/N 50°--N 25°).

- *No punctuation* is used between the end of the scale statement and the beginning of subfield "c" (see the exceptions below).
- *Subfield "c" is not used* in the 034 field (it is obsolete).
- When field 255 ends with a closing parenthesis, it is acceptable to add a period to complete the line even though this creates a "double punctuation" situation.

034 1 a |b 250000 |d W0063000 |e E0101500 |f N0280000 |g N0174500
255   Scale 1:250,000 |c (W 6°30'--E 10°15'/N 28°00'--N 17°45').

034 1 a |b 100000 |d E0154730 |e E0381000 |f S0055510 |g S0352249
255   Scale ca. 1:100,000 |c (E 15°47'30"--E 38°10'00"/S 5°55'10"--S 35°22'49").

034 3 a |b 12000 |b 28000
255   Scale 1:12,000--1:28,000

034 3 a |b 75000 |b 1000
255   Scale 1:75,000. Vertical scale 1:1,000.

FIGURE 11.4. Examples of 255 Field Situations, Including the 034 Field and Its Coding for Comparison (*Source:* WorldCat Database, the OCLC Online Union Catalog [WorldCat], see <http://www.oclc.org/firstsearch/database/details/dbinformation_WorldCat.html>.)

find that the RF is 1:253,440. Many times a calculator is not handy or available, such as when you are looking through maps in a drawer in the map collection, and knowing what to do with 63360, even with paper and pencil, makes life easier.

PROJECTION INFORMATION

This area of the 255 field, subfield "b", or the Statement of projection area, is the easiest to transcribe. Rule 3.3C1 in AACR2R says to give a statement of projection if it is found on the item, its container, or in accompanying textual material. Therefore, if a Statement of projection is *not* found in any of these sources, then the cataloger moves on to providing coordinates.

If, however, a projection statement is found on the item, etc., then provide it, but also do the following:

1. Use abbreviations that are appropriate, most especially the word "projection" may be shortened to "proj.", and numerals are used in place of words.
2. Capitalize proper names such as "Mercator" and "Lambert" when they are a part of the statement.
3. *Optionally add* associated phrases that are a part of the projection statement, such as those relating to standard parallels used, the location of a central meridian on the map, or the centered position of a place (but do not add statements of ellipsoid; instead give these in a note, if warranted).

In addition, *be sure to code the corresponding Projection fixed field* according to the type of projection named in this field. A list of corresponding codes to projections can be found online at <http://lcweb. loc.gov/marc/bibliographic/ecbd008s.html> or in OCLC's *Bibliographic Formats and Standards* in the "Proj" fixed field area.

STATEMENT OF COORDINATES

One of the least-understood concepts in cataloging maps is that of coordinates. Coordinates allow one to find a specific point on the Earth's surface or to identify a geographic area by listing a set of coordinates that enclose the area in question. A two-point set of coordinates that identifies a specific point on the Earth's surface is generically known as a "center point" or "coordinate point," which might be used to identify a point of elevation or location of a city on a small-scale map, for instance. In terms of map cataloging, however, we need to provide "bounding coordinates," a set of four coordinate points that surround a geographic area, such as a county, state, country, or continent. Naturally, these can also identify a nonpolitical entity, such as a geographic region of any size. With sheet maps, four coordinate points are identified and given, and they typically form a rectangle or square (but can also be other shapes) known as the "bounding box," in which the interior contains the geographic area that has been mapped (see Figure 11.5).

Let me note here that it is optional in current map cataloging practice to give coordinates in the bibliographic record whether they appear on the map or can be determined from other sources. This is why Rule 3.3D in AACR2R does not go any further in detail than asking the cataloger to give coordinates. This makes the interpretations for this rule as established in *Cartographic Materials* extremely important.

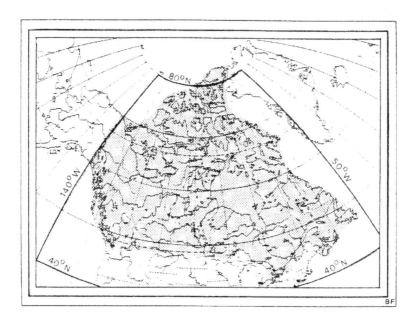

Coordinates. Map has varying degrees of detail
(W 141°—W 50°/N 85°—N 42°)

FIGURE 11.5. Bounding Box Coordinates (*Source:* Reproduced from *Cartographic Materials: A Manual of Interpretation for the AACR2,* 1982, p. 60. Permission granted by the American Library Association.)

Although it is optional within AACR2R rules, current practice also dictates that one should provide a set of bounding coordinates when they do appear on the map, whether they appear at the corners of the map or have to be extrapolated to form the bounding box around the extent of the mapped geographic area. This author would urge everyone to provide coordinates in the bibliographic record whether or not they are given on the map. The reason for this plea is that this very powerful means of describing a geographic area, using coordinates, allows for retrieval of all maps and other cartographic items that include all or part of the area in question. It is said that at least 80 percent of all information, no matter its form, has a geographic link to one or more places. The Alexandria Digital Library's search engine has allowed this kind of retrieval by bounding coordinates of maps and other geo-coded items, such as aerial photographs and satellite images, since the early 1990s. In addition, new software functions built into Endeavor's Integrated Library System, called Voyager, allow those libraries operating on Voyager the power to retrieve maps and, for that matter, any other type of material similarly geo-coded using coordinates. Thus, the importance of providing this piece of information in the record is greatly enhanced. Imagine the power of attaching place to monographs, artworks, serials, musical works, and all other forms of information, not the least of which is cartographic, and being able to allow library patrons to retrieve information on a cross-format basis!

Latitude and Longitude, or North and South versus East and West

One must understand the grid network imposed on the Earth's surface first before the idea of coordinates can be fully comprehended. Discussions of the equator and prime meridian and latitude, longitude, and height can be found at Peter H. Dana's Coordinate Systems Overview Web site at <http://www.colorado. edu/geography/gcraft/notes/coordsys/coordsys_f.html> (click on "Coordinate Systems" in the left-hand list of links), but allow me to summarize the concept of latitude and longitude.

Imagine the Earth in its three-dimensional form, basically a large ball. The line drawn around its middle is known as the equator. Anything located above that line is said to exist in the north and therefore exists in the northern *latitude*. Anything located below that line is said to exist in the south and therefore exists in the southern *latitude.* Thus, north and south are born and points or areas in either of these regions are located in the northern latitudes or southern latitudes. Lines circling the width of the Earth and parallel to the equator are called parallels. The equator is the zero-degree parallel, and each line drawn above or below the equator is progressively larger in number until you reach one of the poles, at which time you reach ninety degrees north or south (i.e., the north pole or south pole).

Similarly, a single line drawn around the Earth from top to bottom, or pole to pole, distinguishes the cardinal directions of east and west. Anything located to the left of that line would be considered to exist in the west, and anything to the right of that line would be considered to exist in the east. Moving away from the line to either the left (west) or right (east) means that you are traveling *longitudinally,* or along lines of increasing or decreasing *longitude,* as each of these lines can be drawn from pole to pole. Each line of longitude is called a meridian. The starting point, or zero degrees of longitude, is known as the prime meridian; it passes through Greenwich, England, and so is also known as the Greenwich prime meridian or the Greenwich meridian.

How to Record Coordinates in the Bibliographic Record

Back to providing geographic coordinates in the bibliographic record. If we are going to provide a set of four coordinates, we must do so in some kind of specific order; to do so randomly would defeat the purpose of allowing anyone to read and understand this set of information. Therefore, a methodology was developed that allows for a specific order in which to provide each coordinate, and, once learned, the cataloger can easily transfer this ordered set of coordinates into a mental image of the area of the Earth's surface, wherever that might be. Rule 3.3D1 in AACR2R and Rule 3D1a in *Cartographic Materials* describe this order:

> westernmost extent of the area covered by the item (longitude); (i.e., the leftmost side of the area)
> easternmost extent of the area covered by the item (longitude); (i.e., the rightmost side of the area)
> northernmost extent of the area covered by the item (latitude); (i.e., the topmost side of the area)
> southernmost extent of the area covered by the item (latitude); (i.e., the bottommost side of the area)

This order must be followed no matter what region of the Earth is being considered, and when working with maps that are outside of the northern latitudes (i.e., north of the Earth's equator) and western longitudes (i.e., west of the Greenwich meridian), the task can become confusing. For example, much of the continent of Africa is in the southern latitudes and eastern longitudes, and the bounding coordinates might typically be denoted as so many degrees east by so many degrees east by so many degrees south by so many degrees south. This differs from places in the United States or Canada, which would have north-by-north and west-by-west coordinates. *Always remember* west first, east second, north third, and south last, or left first, right second, top third, and bottom last, and you will never go wrong! The following are some examples of bounding coordinates of countries around the globe, expressed in mathematical form:

United States (excluding Alaska and Hawaii):
   (W 125°--W 65°/N 49°--N 25°)
Panama: (W 83°--W 77°/N 10°--N 7°)
Sweden: (E 11°--E 24°/N 70°--N 55°)
Ethiopia: (E 32°--E 48°/N 17°--N 3°)
Japan: (E 123°--E 148°/N 46°--N 24°)
Philippines: (E 117°--E 127°/N 19°--N 4°)
Australia: (E 112°--E 155°/S 10°--S 45°)

Examples of countries that either straddle the equator or the prime meridian and thus have a mixture of west-and-east or north-and-south coordinate pairs include these:

England and Wales: (W 6°--E 2°/N 56°--N 49°)
Brazil: (W 74°--W 34°/N 5°--S 34°)
Algeria: (W 8°--E 12°/N 37°--N 19°)

Did you know that one of our continents straddles both the equator and prime meridian?

Africa: (W 20°--E 60°/N 40°--S 50°)

Equally as important as giving the correct order of bounding coordinates is expressing these in their mathematical form, for this form is much more concise in its application than the same information expressed linguistically. (Proof of this is found in the paragraph preceding the list of countries and their coordinates!) This also takes some practice before it is both understood and expressed accurately and consistently, but it is important, so that anyone looking at this information can interpret it correctly. Rule 3D1b in *Cartographic Materials* states:

> Express the coordinates in degrees . . . , minutes . . . , and seconds of the sexagesimal system (360-degree circle) taken from the Greenwich prime meridian. . . . Precede each coordinate by W, E, N, or S, as appropriate. Separate the two sets of latitude and longitude by a [forward] diagonal slash, and separate each longitude or latitude from its counterpart by a dash.

Rule 3D1b(3) in *Cartographic Materials* does specify providing bounding coordinates in one of two ways: "For items where the surrounding area is not treated in the same degree of detail, record the coordinates, a) for the four corners, or b) for the significant or principal mapped area. (See Fig. 6)". "Fig. 6" (Figure 11.5 in this chapter) is an excellent visualization of part "b" of this application to Rule 3D1b(3), showing all of Canada plus Greenland and Alaska; the bounding coordinates would be for the country of Canada, and, therefore, the land masses and oceans to the west and east of Canada would not apply.

Also very important in this process of listing coordinates is the need to be uniform in doing so. Thus, aim to provide not only the simplest set possible but also a consistent set based on degrees, minutes, and seconds. Think of the possibilities of sets of bounding coordinates as falling into one of three potential outcomes: a set that has coordinates only at the degrees level, a set that has coordinates at the degrees-minutes level, and a set that has coordinates at the degrees-minutes-seconds level (see Box 11.1). Whether provided at one of these three levels, or formats, if you will, or extrapolated by the cataloger, a consistent level must be attained, and as the last sentence in the APPLICATION to Rule 3D1b states, "[s]upply zeros where necessary to ensure consistency." This means that if even one coordinate contains information at the degrees-minutes level or degrees-minutes-seconds level when the other coordinates contain information at only the degrees or degrees-minutes level, one must supply zeros to indicate the next lowest level of information, either for minutes or for minutes and seconds.

BOX 11.1. Examples of Bounding Coordinate Set Situations

Once again, there are two general rules of thumb to follow:

1. The level of order of degrees, minutes, and seconds must be consistent across subfield "c" in the 255 field, i.e., all degrees, all degrees and minutes, or all degrees, minutes, and seconds, using zero as a place holder where necessary.
2. Numbers must match between scale/coordinates given in the 255 field and those given in the 034 field.

034 1 a |b 1000000 |d W1250000 |e W0650000 |f N0500000 |g N0250000
255   Scale 1:1,000,000 |c (W 125°--W 65°/N 50°--N 25°).

- *No punctuation* is used between the end of the scale statement and the beginning of subfield "c" (see the exceptions below).
- *Subfield "c" is not used* in the 034 field (it is obsolete).
- When field 255 ends with a closing parenthesis, it is acceptable to add a period to complete the line even though this creates a "double punctuation" situation.

034 1 a |b 250000 |d W0063000 |e E0101500 |f N0280000 |g N0174500
255   Scale 1:250,000 |c (W 6°30'--E 10°15'/N 28°00'--N 17°45').

034 1 a |b 100000 |d E0154730 |e E0381000 |f S0055510 |g S0352249
255   Scale ca.1:100,000 |c (E 15°47'30"--E 38°10'00"/S 5°55'10"--S 35°22'49").

Not: 255 Scale 1:50,000 |c (W 82°30'--W 76°/N 33°20'05"--N 30°10'), as this shows a mixture of levels of degrees, minutes, and seconds.

Punctuation exception: The only two times that punctuation is used between the end of the scale statement and the beginning of the coordinates statement, or subfield "c", in the 255 field is to provide a period immediately following the scale statement and before wording of an equivalent verbal scale or other wording and/or providing a semicolon following the scale statement but before a statement of projection using the space-semicolon-space convention. Examples include:

255 Scale 1:744,080. 1 in. = 28 miles ; |b transverse Mercator proj. |c (W 80°--W 75°/N 42° --N 40°).
255 Scale 1:10,000 ; |b polyconic proj. |c (W 55°--W 48°/N 48°--N 32°).

This same level of consistency in providing bounding coordinate information in the coded mathematical variable field (034) is also achieved using zeros, and the information is even more explicit in that, for each coordinate, seven digits must be supplied after each cardinal direction (W for west, E for east, N for north, and S for south).

Extrapolating Bounding Coordinates

Oftentimes you will find that coordinates are given on the map but they either do not extend to the corners of the map or do not fall outside the boundary of the geographic area in question in one or more of the four directions. In such cases the cataloger is required to make some educated guesses based on the coordinates that are available on the map; this is called "extrapolating" the bounding coordinates. Although not a complicated exercise, it does take some practice to get comfortable with making extrapolations. I recommend pulling a small number of Central Intelligence Agency (CIA) maps from your collection to use for practice. CIA maps typically do have coordinates, but they most usually do not cover the geographic area in one or more directions and thus make good practice examples (see Figure 11.6).

The primary goal of providing coordinates for any sheet map is to make sure that they create a "bounding box" around the geographic area that is the main map. Whereas AACR2R's Rule 3.3D1 does not go into specifics regarding the capture of a geographic area within a coordinate box, the APPLICATION FOR SPECIFIC CASES to Rule 3D1b in *Cartographic Materials* does, and it also includes other situations relating to coordinates for sheet maps. In particular, number four in this list specifies that "[w]hen the coordinates printed on the item do not extend to the neat line or edge of the item, establish them as precisely as possible by extrapolation." Figure 11.7 shows just such a situation for the West Indies and the Caribbean where the coordinates cut across the geographic area in all four directions. Note that it is okay to give the limit of coordinates in any of the four directions on a map even if they include more than the specified geographic area for the title being cataloged, but, preferably, one should aim to extrapolate only to the greatest extent of the geographic detail, as opposed to aiming for the edges of the map itself.

To begin the extrapolation process, first note the level of detail of the coordinates given: Are they given as only whole degrees, degrees and minutes, or degrees, minutes, and seconds? In the majority of cases, the coordinates already on the map are in whole degrees, making the process relatively straightforward. Next, determine how many degrees apart two or more lines of latitude or longitude are by reviewing or counting from one line to the next. For instance, if one line of latitude is at ten degrees and the next one given to either its north or

FIGURE 11.6. CIA Map of the Former Yugoslavia Republics (*Source:* <http://www.lib.utexas.edu/maps/europe/western_balkans.jpg>. *Note:* Extrapolate to the left and right for longitude coordinates [meridians]; extrapolate to the top and bottom for latitude coordinates [parallels].)

south is twenty degrees, then the distance between these is ten degrees. Note that if the distance between these two lines of latitude is ten degrees, it is easy to determine a length of five degrees (one-half the distance between the two lines) or even smaller degree segments. Thus, extrapolating using whole degree designations is the simplest way to accomplish this task, although it certainly does not prevent one from extrapolating to the minutes or even seconds level, which would provide a more exact boundary.

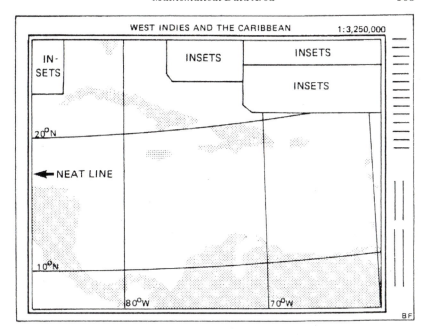

Coordinates, extrapolated to neat line
(W 86°—W 60°/N 27°—N 7°)

FIGURE 11.7. Extrapolated Coordinates (*Source:* Reproduced from *Cartographic Materials: A Manual of Interpretation for the AACR2,* 1982, p. 61. Permission granted by the American Library Association.)

Based on this knowledge, and starting with the line of latitude (or longitude) closest to one of the neat lines or edges of the map, determine, either by measuring with a ruler or by eyeballing the distance involved, the approximate distance from the line to the neat line or edge. Depending on which quadrant of the Earth is involved, either add or subtract the approximated distance to the line of latitude or longitude. In other words, if the geographic area involved is north of the equator and west of the prime meridian and you are extrapolating a coordinate based on a line of latitude on the western (lefthand side), then you would *add* the distance to the westernmost meridian to extrapolate to the westernmost portion of the geographic area or the neat line or border. However, if you need to determine the eastern (righthand side) meridian, then you would *subtract* the extrapolated distance from the easternmost meridian to the neat line or border. To determine the northern (top) boundary you would again *add* the extrapolated distance to the northernmost parallel and *subtract* from the southernmost parallel to determine the southern (bottom) boundary.

Also, be careful to notice where on the Earth's surface this quadrant is located, for if one of the lines of longitude crosses over the Greenwich meridian (zero-degree line of longitude), you may have to change the cardinal direction in your coordinates statement from east to west or west to east; similarly, if your new line of latitude crosses over the equator (zero-degree line of latitude), you may have to change the coordinates statement for that particular direction from north to south or south to north.

Once you have completed one direction in this manner, move on to the next one, if necessary. Remember that the process may entail only one line of latitude or longitude and moving it outward in a particular direction, or it may involve two or more of these lines. When you have completed the extrapolation process, ask yourself whether the coordinate "box" around the geographic area contains that area completely—if it does not on one or more of the sides, then further extrapolation is needed.

Representative Fraction Only

Scale 1:25,000

Albers Equal Area Projection

SCALE 1:5,000,000

1:100 000-scale metric topographic map

Representative Fraction Only (in a Different Language)

ESCALA 1/100000

Limites intermunicipais conforme o dec lei 4505 de 30.12.943

Sondeado por: Secc. Hidrografía	
Elaborado	por: Abdón Inciarte M.
Dibujado	
Escala = 1: 50. 000	

Representative Fraction and Bar Scale

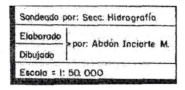

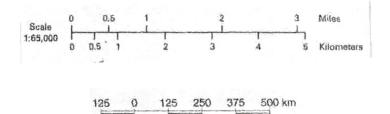

The scale is 1:10,780,000

FIGURE 11.8. Samples of Types of Scales Taken from Actual Maps

Representative Fraction with Additional Scale Information

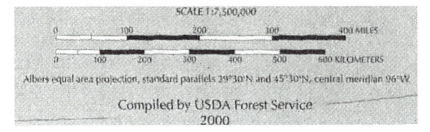

Verbal (or Stated) Scale Statement

SCALE - 1" = 100'

1 inch = 1,430 feet

Voting Precincts for the
City of Williamsport

Verbal (or Stated) Scale Statement and Bar Scale

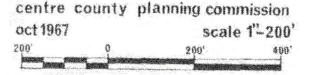

FIGURE 11.8 *(continued)*

Bar Scale Only (in Miles)

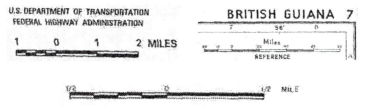

Bar Scale Only (in Feet)

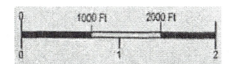

Bar Scale Only (in Kilometers)

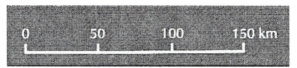

Bar Scale Only (in Multiple Measurements)

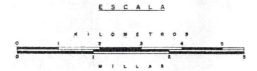

FIGURE 11.8 *(continued)*

Chapter 12

Publication Information

Providing publication information for a map is similar in nature to the same process with cataloging monographs or other types of formats, although very often a publication statement is not available or is incomplete in terms of lacking a place or date of publication. According to AACR2R, the Prescribed source of information for the "Publication, distribution, etc." area for a map is the Chief source of information, i.e., the map itself or any accompanying printed material. In other words, if a publication statement is found anywhere on the map sheet or accompanying material, then it can be used in the bibliographic record.

The trouble with maps is that often either they lack a formal publication statement altogether or the cataloger has to ascertain a publication statement based on less than ideal information or information that does not clearly represent the publisher and/or distributor. If the majority of map titles had a formal publication statement, indicated by a phrase such as "Published by . . . ," life would be much easier; however, this simply isn't the case. Therefore, the cataloger must rely on garnering knowledge of the locations of publication statements for the more common map publishers and must also understand that most map producers also publish their own materials. Since the most difficult part of discerning publication information relates to the date(s) of publication, as well as the difference between date of publication and date of situation, much of the following discussion will focus on this area.

PLACE OF PUBLICATION

The rule in Chapter 3 of AACR2R for this area refers the cataloger to the rules in 1.4C in Chapter 1. This part of the area is pretty straightforward; if the place of publication is on the map, then transcribe it as such in the 260 subfield "a" area, maintaining both the form (language) and grammatical case as they appear. The most common problem is lack of a place of publication. The second most common problem is a change of place over time as a particular company either was bought out by another company or simply moved from one location to another during its history. Both of these problems are not insurmountable; in fact, oftentimes an authority record for the company may include an indication of where the company is and/or was located. In addition, reference sources about companies abound in research libraries and may include anything from telephone directories to works about publishing companies to company histories. For existing companies, the Internet is a quick and easy resource for most of us. Thankfully, the longer a company has been in existence, the better the chance that if a recent map lacks a place of publication, an earlier map from the same company likely will have the place on it.

Perhaps, as mentioned earlier, the best resource of all is simply working with maps over a period of time or, lacking this kind of experience, actually going into a map collection and getting a sample of a company or agency's maps that cover a significant time period. Some garnering of this kind of knowledge is simply common sense. For example, if the map is produced and/or published by one of a country's federal mapmaking agencies, then it is safe to assume that the agency resides in the country's capital. The same can be said for state, provincial, or territorial mapmaking agencies. Private mapmaking companies can be somewhat more difficult, but you will quickly learn that, for instance, Rand McNally and Company originally was located in Chicago, then relocated to Skokie, Illinois, in the 1980s, and is headquartered there today. Any place information derived in this manner will need to be bracketed since the source of information was not on the item itself.

At the very least, according to Rule 1.4C6, if a particular city isn't given, a probable place of publication may be supplied, in square brackets and with a question mark. This is often used when the place of publication is not found on the map or any accompanying material but the cataloger's general knowledge about the company or agency makes an educated guess worthwhile. For example, so many U.S. federal agencies reside in or near Washington, DC, that a map produced or published by the Federal Highway Administration with no place of publication given could reasonably be assumed to have been published in Washington, DC; this would be given as "[Washington, D.C.?]" in the record.

If a probable place of publication cannot be determined, the next part of Rule 1.4C6 says to supply the name of the country, state, province, territory, etc., in which the map likely was published, again using square brackets. Add a question mark within the square brackets if you are not certain about the place of publication even at the country, state, etc., level.

Finally, if all else fails, give the Latin phrase for "without place," or more generically no local place, *sine loco,* as an abbreviation and in square brackets, e.g., [S.l.] : |b Big Red Monster Cartography, . . .

NAME OF PUBLISHER, DISTRIBUTOR, ETC.

Rule 3.4D1 in AACR2R refers us to Rule 1.4D for instructions on how to provide the name of the publisher or distributor. According to Rule 1.4D1, we are to give the name of the publisher following the place to which it relates. We may also provide the name of the publisher or distributor in the shortest form in which it can still be understood internationally to be the name of a publisher or distributor; therefore, we can abbreviate such words as "Company," and "Department," and "Division" or drop a term of incorporation. Further, according to Rule 1.4D3, we do not drop words indicating function, such as "Printed for . . ." or "Distributed by . . . ," from the statement of publisher.

If two or more agencies are named as performing the same function, list the first-named agency but also give the second agency if it is given prominence on the map. This is done by concluding the first place of publication/name of publisher area with a space semicolon space, giving a second place of publication to match the second prominently named publisher, then space colon space and the name of the second publisher. *Or,* if both publishers are associated with the same place of publication, simply follow the first publisher with space colon space and the name of the second publisher. Examples of both of these situations follow:

Chicago : |b Rand McNally and Co. ; |a Convent Station, N.J. :
   |b General Drafting Co., |c 1957.
New York : |b Kaiser Handi-Book Publishers : |b Yellow
   Book Co., |c 1963.

What can we do if no publisher, distributor, etc., is given on the map?
Rule 14.D7 says that "[i]f the name of the publisher, distributor, etc.,
is unknown, give *s.n.* (sine nomine) or its equivalent in a nonroman
script."

London : |b [s.n.], |c [192-?]
[S.l. : |b s.n., |c 19--?]

Finally, if doubt exists about whether the named company or agency
is a publisher or a manufacturer, treat it as a publisher according to
Rule 1.4D8.

PUBLICATION DATE

Once again the rule in Chapter 3 of AACR2R refers us to Chapter 1
for applying the publication date for the map. The rules in Area 1.4F
cover more than a half dozen provisions for publication date, beginning with 1.4F1: "For published items, give the date (i.e., year) of
publication, distribution, etc., of the edition, revision, etc., named in
the edition area. If there is no edition statement, give the date of the
first publication of the edition to which the item belongs." Also,
"Give dates in Western-style arabic numerals. If the date found in the
item is not of the Gregorian or Julian calendar, give the date as found
and follow it with the year(s) of the Gregorian or Julian calendar."
   A couple of the rules that often are applied because they relate to
the circumstances surrounding the publication of a map have to do
with copyright dates. According to Rule 1.4F5, which is an optional
addition to the rules previous to this, one may add the latest date of
copyright following the date of publication if they differ. Most often
for maps falling into this category, it is a single copyright date. In addition, Rule 1.4F6 says that if the item lacks a publication or distribution date but does have a copyright date, then provide the copyright
date as the date of publication, and as a last resort, if no publication,
distribution, or copyright dates are available and a date of manufac-

ture is, then provide the date of manufacture in their place, indicating it by a term such as "printing" following the given date. The first half of Rule 1.4F6 is a common occurrence for commercially published maps.

The Common Problem of No Publication Date

The most common publication date situation for maps is simply not having one to provide! This is one of those many minor irritations when working with maps, and if it is not the publication date that is lacking, then it is the publisher or place of publication or scale or some combination of various pieces of information. Rule 1.4F7 addresses the "completely lacking a date" situation: "If no date of publication . . . appears in an item, supply an approximate date of publication." This is where *Cartographic Materials* once again proves its extreme value because it provides some clear examples of how to infer a date of publication when this information is lacking. First, the APPLICATION to Rule 4F1 in CM about a lacking date of publication notes that "a publication date can often be inferred from other information appearing on the cartographic item. Enclose inferred dates in square brackets. If it is doubtful that the inferred date is the actual publication date, add a question mark within the square brackets." A list of sources that may provide an inferred publication date follows the APPLICATION, including these:

- A date in the title proper, other title information, or alternate title
- A date in the statement of responsibility
- A date in the edition statement other than an edition date, such as a date of revision
- A printing or publisher's code (Some examples are included in Chapter 14, "Notes in the Record.")
- Other information appearing elsewhere on the item, e.g., the date of population statistics given at the head of an index to cities and towns, a date of estimated population, or a phrase or combination of phrases in an advertisement

Following this list of examples is a list of items that should *not* be used in attempting to derive an inferred date of publication, which is just as valuable as the previous list! Likewise, the APPLICATION to Rule 4F7 in CM is helpful and encouraging: "Use publishers' lists and catalogues, and printed bibliographies if special searching for a more precise publication date is desired," when no date of publication, manufacture, or copyright is available to use.

Finally, Rule 1.4F8 of AACR2R has to do with providing a range of dates or an open date for circumstances involving two or more dates appearing on various parts of an item. For maps, this would be specific to a map series. If opening and closing dates of publication can be determined then provide both separated by a dash; however, if the map set or series is not yet complete, then provide the opening date followed by a hyphen, without a space, to indicate that the title is still active.

Publication Date versus Date of Situation (or "Situation Date")

Although more specific date-of-situation information can be found in Chapter 15, "Classification Using the LC G-Schedule," do not underestimate the importance of understanding the difference between the date of publication versus date of situation. Thus, I broach this topic as part of the Date of publication, distribution, etc. area in order to ensure that the difference in date types is apparent early in the discussion of cataloging sheet maps.

First, with experience, you will find that the publication date most often is the same date used in the call number and de facto also becomes the date of situation, only because no other information on the map indicates the date(s) on which the cartographic information was created. However, if the cartographic information was created at an earlier time than that in which the map was published, the date of creation (or the "date of information" as LC calls it) is the date of situation, and the date used in the call number. For example, text that accompanies the map titled "The Nordic Countries from Satellite" indicates that the image shown is a mosaic of satellite images taken by a LANDSAT satellite orbiting the Earth between the years 1978 and 1980. The map itself was copyrighted and published in 1981. Obviously, the publication date is 1981, but the date of situation, the one used in the call number, is 1980 because the last cartographic information was collected in that year. See Figure 12.1 for the record for this title.

OCLC: 20174930 Rec stat: c

Entered: 19890814 Replaced: 20010724 Used: 20010724

Type: e ELvl: I Srce: d Relf: Ctrl: Lang: swe

BLvl: m Form: GPub: f SpFm: MRec: Ctry: sw

CrTp: a Indx: 0 Proj: DtSt: s Dates: 1981,

Desc: a

1	040	GZN |c GZN |d OCL |d UPM
2	007	a |b j |d a |e a |f n |g z |h n
3	034 1	a |b 2000000 |d E0020000 |e E0320000 |f N0720000 |g N0500000
4	041	swenordanfineng
5	043	ev-----
6	052	6911
7	090	G6911.A4 1980 |b .F4
8	090	|b
9	049	UPMM
10	110 2	Njellanger Wider²e AS.

11 245 10 Norden frèan satellit : |b satellitkartan èar framstèalld 1981 = The Nordic countries from satellite / |c i samarbete mellan de nordiska lèanderna, Fjellanger Wider²e AS ; Lantmèateriet.

12 255 Scale 1:2,000,000 |c (E 2°--E 32°/N 72°--N 50°).

13 260 Trondheim, [Sweden] : |b Fjellanger Wider²e AS ; |a Gèavle, [Sweden] : |b Lantmèateriet, |c [1981]

14 300 1 map ; |c on sheet 103 x 86 cm.

15 500 Also shows Iceland.

16 500 "The mosaic has been assembled from approximately 200 satellite images which have been registered by the American earth resource satellites LANDSAT 1978-1980."

17 500 "Registering: NASA. Signalmottagning och negativframstèallning, Rymdbolaget. Bildframstèallning och sammansèattning, Lantmèateriet, 1981."

18 500 "Copyright: Lantmèateriverket, 801 12 Gèavle."

19 500 Includes text, notes, and outline map of Iceland, Norway, Sweden, and Finland.

20 546 Text in Swedish, Norwegian, Danish, Finnish and English.

21 651 0 Scandinavia |v Remote-sensing maps.

22 710 1 Sweden. |b Statens lantmèateriverk.

23 710 2 Rymdbolaget.

FIGURE 12.1. Example of Date of Situation in the Call Number versus Publication Date (*Source:* WorldCat Database, the OCLC Online Union Catalog [WorldCat], see <http://www.oclc.org/firstsearch/database/details/dbinformation_ WorldCat.html>.)

TRACING FOR CARTOGRAPHIC PUBLISHER

A final point to consider, one that differs from some other formats, is that it is acceptable to trace for the name of a publisher, if the person, company, or agency is known to be a regular provider/producer of cartographic materials. See Chapter 17, "Added Entries in the Record," for further details on this aspect.

Chapter 13

Physical Description Area

This is the second area of the bibliographic record that causes great concern to catalogers who are new to working with sheet maps and to those who catalog maps on an irregular basis. Nothing is complicated about any of the parts of the 300 field, but the cataloger must be aware of many situations and able to provide accurate descriptions for them. To some "variety is the spice of life," as the old saying goes, but to others the possibilities for physical description amount to a major headache. Most troublesome it seems is the concept of the "neat line" as the basis for providing measured dimensions for the map(s); we delve into this further later in this chapter. Other troublesome areas include which map(s) is(are) to be described (what is the "main map" and what other maps are not), correctly counting the maps involved, and dealing with "both sides" versus "back to back," all of which is explained in detail shortly. After reviewing cartographic Specific Material Designations we examine the three primary subfield areas within the 300 field one at a time to discern the various aspects involved within each.

TERMINOLOGY

Before we move ahead, though, an introduction to, and clarification of, terminology regarding multiple maps on multiple sheets is necessary. Map titles are published in multiple physical sheets as well as on single sheets, and once we encounter multiple physical sheets, each with a map printed on it, the physical description of the title becomes more complex. Details regarding how to proceed with the "Extent of item" area and the "Dimensions" area follow in the sections Two or More Maps on Two or More Sheets and, later, Two or More Maps on Multiple Sheets. First, let's review some terms and their meanings.

Map Sets, Map Series, Multisheet Maps, and Related Situations

What is meant by the terms "multisheet map," "map set," "map series," and "collection" in the context of any map title that is produced on more than one sheet? The most straightforward of these four concepts is "multisheet map." This is a single monographic map printed on multiple physical sheets because of the size of the geographic area shown at a relatively large scale. Some clear indications of when one has a multisheet map in hand are described here in the following text, but the key idea is that no single sheet can stand alone bibliographically—the combining of the physical sheets must occur for the title to be described correctly. *Cartographic Materials,* in the APPLICATION to Rule 5B, uses the term "sheets" to describe this situation. This is the exact opposite of what can occur with the other three terms; in the case of map sets, map series, or collections, each individual sheet may possibly be cataloged separately, although that is not usually the intent of the published group of maps.

The most common generic term used to describe a cartographic title that contains multiple maps on multiple sheets is "map set." The term "map set" is used to mean "map series," "multipart map," or "collection" by those individuals, including myself, who use this label; for clarity, however, it will not be used in the discussions in this chapter or elsewhere in the book because "map set" is not used or formally recognized in AACR2R or other cataloging manuals due to the confusion it often causes. Velma Parker (1999), "Cataloguing Map Series and Serials," states that map set "is often considered a synonym for map series." Others may also use the label "map series" as a synonym in the same manner to cover those titles in which the maps are part of a collective group or set but are not part of a formal series. For the purposes of this book, when discussing what are physically similar items, although not always bibliographically alike, the terms "map series" and "collection" are used henceforth.

"Map series" encompasses those titles which are monographic in nature (i.e., a single record is created to describe the title) but have been published as a series and include a mechanism for keeping the individual maps in order, most usually a numbering or alphanumeric system. Parker (1999) indicates that all map series have been described and categorized accordingly as follows:

- *Contiguous-area series:* The intent is for all of the sheets, when joined together, to cover an entire country at one scale.
- *Same area but different themes series:* A particular geographic area, most usually a state, province, territory, or country, is shown on each sheet, but each sheet displays a different theme or subject.
- *Different areas but same theme series:* This is the opposite of the previous series; one theme or subject is shown on different geographic areas.
- *Successively numbered or repetitively titled series:* Usually the group of maps covers one geographic area, much as in the contiguous-area series, but the sheet lines are not regular, as in the contiguous-area series, and coverage may be at different scales.
- *Part of a book series:* The maps involved are produced in tandem with the books in the book series.

The aforementioned work by Velma Parker is the best source for cataloging map series and serials, and Appendix E in *Cartographic Materials* is also helpful in regard to map series. Figure 13.6 provides an excellent visual illustration of this concept as well, although it may also represent a map "collection" or group that is not part of a formal map series.

The last category of terms to be discussed is the "collection" or multipart map, which is labeled as "parts" in CM in the APPLICATION to Rule 5B. A "part" is defined in CM as

> a physically separate unit that can stand alone bibliographically. It may be used in conjunction with other units of similar design, e.g., a group of maps each of a common area but displaying various themes; or, a group of maps designed primarily for use individually or to provide total coverage of a specific area.

Note that this definition covers several of the types of map series given earlier. Again, physically, a "collection" is the same as a map series in that multiple maps on multiple sheets are involved and they often are numbered and of the same scale, but in this case the title is not part of a formal series. An example of a map "collection" would be the title "[Mexico's states]"; this is a group of thirty-two maps, each of which covers one state in Mexico and in this case at different scales, as seen in the following bibliographic record:

```
OCLC: 47757691        Rec stat:  n
Entered: 20010810  Replaced: 20010810   Used: 20010810
Type: e   ELvl: I   Srce: d   Relf: ak      Ctrl:        Lang: spa
BLvl: m   Form:     GPub: u   SpFm:         MRec:        Ctry: mx
CrTp: b   Indx: 0   Proj:     DtSt: s       Dates: 1968,
Desc: a
 1 040     UPM |c UPM
 2 007     a |b j |d a |e a |f n |g z |h n
 3 034     0 a |d W1180000 |e W0860000 |f N0330000 |g N0140000
 4 043     n-mx---
 5 052     4411
 6 090     G4411.F7 svar |b .M4
 7 090     |b
 8 049     UPMM
 9 245 00 [Mexico's states] |h [map]
10 255     Scales differ |c (W 118°--W 86°/N 33°--N 14°).
11 260     [Mexico City? : |b s.n., |c 1968?]
12 300     maps ; |c 55 x 55 cm. or smaller, on sheets 49 x 72 cm. or
smaller.
13 500     Title supplied by cataloger.
14 500     Relief shown by contours. Depths shown by isolines.
15 500     Each sheet covers one state, separately titled using state name.
16 500     Stamped on: G&M Division, June 1968.
17 500     Each sheet individually numbered.
18 500     Includes indexed ancillary map showing political subdivisions
and ill. Some sheets include insets of major metropolitan areas.
19 650 0  Mexico |x Administrative and political divisions |v Maps.
20 651 0  Mexico |v Maps.
```

Note that each map is individually titled, so, theoretically, if access were needed at the state level for this group of maps, it could be done. However, the individual sheets when brought together form a "collection" under one unifying title (even though it is provided in this case by the cataloger), it is a group or set of maps intended to be used together.

To reiterate, whenever a discussion is about multiple maps on more than one sheet in this book, as opposed to one or more maps on *a single sheet,* the terms "map series" or "collection" are used.

CARTOGRAPHIC SPECIFIC MATERIAL
DESIGNATIONS (SMDs)

The list of special material designations for cartographic materials recently changed. The following list of SMDs must be used in describing the cartographic item being cataloged:

atlas
diagram (e.g., a block diagram)
globe
map
model (e.g., a three-dimensional raised-relief plastic map)
profile
remote-sensing image
section (e.g., a geologic section or cross-section)
view (e.g., a panoramic view or bird's-eye view)

For the purpose of this book, the SMD of "map," highlighted in the previous list, is the one to use when cataloging sheet maps. Please note that the examples given after four of the terms listed are those of the author; they do not appear in the rules themselves. Also, the specific changes to the list in Rule 3.5B1 in AACR2R (1998 Edition and earlier editions) include changing "map section" to "section" and "relief model" to "model," which will both clarify and simplify the terms involved. (Similar in form, but not in fact, are remote-sensing images, defined as actual images of the Earth's surface taken from the air or from space, most usually by airplane, satellite, or space craft. The resulting cartographic image crosses the boundary from remote-sensing image to map whenever additional information, such as place names, grids, or points of elevation, is added directly to the image. A remote-sensing image is just that—the actual image of the Earth's [or other celestial body's] surface without additional information added. *See* HelenJane Armstrong and Jimmie Lundgren's [1999] "Cataloging Aerial Photographs and Other Remote-Sensing Materials," either in *Cataloging & Classification Quarterly* or in the companion book, *Maps and Related Cartographic Materials,* edited by Paige Andrew and Mary Lynette Larsgaard [1999], for details related to cataloging this type of cartographic item.)

How do we handle manuscript maps since the previous list of terms implies designations for machine- or electronically produced maps? Fortunately, the last sentence in Rule 3.5B1 tells us to precede any of the SMDs in the list with the abbreviation "ms." for manuscript, if that is the type of map we are cataloging.

Finally, what does the cataloger do if none of the terms in the SMD list is appropriate to the map(s) being cataloged? After all, it is amazing how many map items, or "cartofacts," are available for purchase and may need to be cataloged for a map or other educational collection. For example, this author has in his office a small metal wastepaper basket with a map of the world on it as well as other map memorabilia, such as map postcards. Again, Rule 3.5B1 does guide us in this circumstance by telling us that if none of the terms in the SMD list "fits" the situation, go to the chapter that does fit and look up the ".5B" rule for that chapter to find the appropriate list of SMDs. A great example given is "52 playing cards." Obviously, each card in the deck has a map on its back, so the cataloger would use Rule 10.5B in the Chapter for "Three-dimensional artifacts and realia" and adapt the "game" SMD to what the actual items are.

HOW MANY MAPS ARE THERE?
(FIELD 300, SUBFIELD "a")

The obvious items, and naturally the ones most easily dealt with, are the "1 map" items involving only one map on one side of the sheet of paper. When the situation involves two or more maps, a single map continued on the back side of the sheet of paper, and/or multiple physical sheets of paper, the work becomes more complicated. Before examining each of these situations one at a time, let us revisit the concept of "main map," as this is the basis for providing an accurate physical description.

The concept of "main map," or "main maps," as the case may be, was described in Chapter 2. To summarize this idea so that we know how many maps are involved and how to proceed with measuring them, first, carefully review the cartographic content of the item to be cataloged to see what appears to be the main map versus any map insets or ancillary maps. Use the idea of "prominence" or "predominance" as a guide during this procedure. As noted in *Cartographic Materials,* under the APPLICATION for Rule 1G2,

> Determine "predominance" on the basis of "publisher's prefer-
> ence" as indicated by relative size and scale of parts; placement
> or prominence of title information; arrangement of constituent
> parts, ancillary maps, etc.; or the relationship between primary
> and supplementary or ancillary maps. (p. 41)

Therefore, rule out insets and ancillary maps noted during the review
process (both are defined in Chapter 2); these are not described in the
Physical Description field but may be denoted in a general note and
possibly given subject access. This will leave you with one or more
main maps to describe. If multiple maps are on the sheet and you have
doubts about which are the main or primary ones, then return to the ti-
tle(s) to try to determine the publisher's intent, looking especially for
subject terms (e.g., "AAA road map of . . ."; "Surficial geology map
of . . ."; ". . . in the age of the dinosaurs"; etc.) as well as geographic
coverage, based on this information. Prominence of words in the title
and/or their prominence based on layout may help to discern the publisher's intent in terms of which is the main map. Most of the time you
will be able to determine confidently just what it is that you are describing in the 300 field between seeing the obvious and using title information as a source of verification. Naturally, as mentioned earlier,
the simplest of all cases is one map on one side of the sheet to be cataloged. Here, we start with the simplest and proceed to the more complex cases.

One Map on One Side of a Single Sheet

> 300   1 map . . .

One Map in Segments on One or Both Sides of a Single Sheet

If a single map is printed in segments but designed to be used as
one map when the segments are fitted together, this remains as "1 map"
and the dimensions given will be of the map as if it were fitted together (see Figure 13.1). In this case, it is important to state also that
this single map is in "pieces," and Rule 3.5B2 of AACR2R says to do
this in one of two ways: (1) give the number of segments involved as
well as the number of maps in the physical description, or (2) give
only the number of maps involved and explain the layout in a separate
note. Cataloger's judgment is invoked here, but it seems clearer to

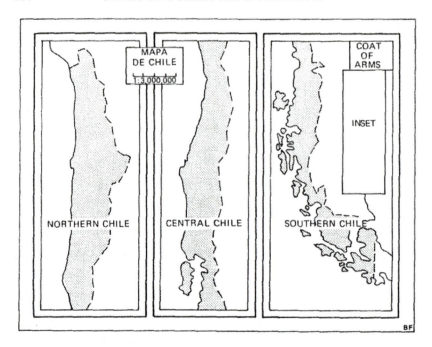

Extent. One map printed in segments on one sheet
1 map . . . *(Explain the layout in a note, if necessary)*

FIGURE 13.1. One Map in Segments on One Sheet (*Source:* Reproduced from
Cartographic Materials: A Manual of Interpretation for the AACR2, 1982, p. 92.
Permission granted by the American Library Association.)

give the number of segments as part of the physical description, for
example:

> 300   1 map in 2 segments . . .

In some cases a single map is in two segments, with each segment
printed on its own side of the sheet; therefore, the map user must start
on one side of the sheet and then turn the sheet over to continue. A
clear indication of this intent is when the publisher provides a visible
"cut line" or includes such wording as "continued on the other side"
at the point where the map continues onto the other side of the sheet
(this can be at the top or bottom or to the left or right) (see Figure 13.2). See the following section for what to do in this case.

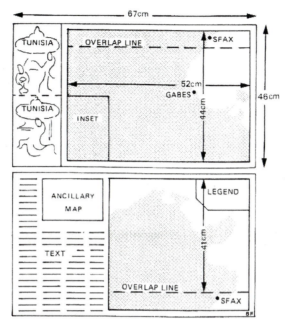

Dimensions. One map continued on verso
1 map: both sides, col; 85 × 52 cm, on sheet 46 × 67 cm

FIGURE 13.2. A Segmented Map on Two Sides of One Sheet (*Source:* Reproduced from *Cartographic Materials: A Manual of Interpretation for the AACR2,* 1982, p. 119. Permission granted by the American Library Association.)

One Map That "Carries Over" to the Other Side of the Sheet

Sometimes, due to the scale chosen for the map compared to the size of the single sheet the map is printed on, the map itself will start on one side of the sheet and finish on the other side. Often the publisher helps us see this by the phrase "continued on other side" at the point where the map leaves off. A less obvious indication is the use of a heavy dashed line across the side of the map where it leaves off, with the neat line or border continuous on the other three sides. A much less obvious indication, one the National Forest Service in particular uses on its maps published in this form, is to leave each side appearing as two separate maps but to show that they join by using a diagram known as a "map key," which is similar to an adjoining-

sheets index (see Figure 13.3, bottom illustration) to indicate this vi-
sually (see Figure 13.3, top illustration). Be aware that, in any of
these cases, the map may leave off at any of the four sides and continue on the other side of the sheet from that point.

    300   1 map : |b both sides . . .

Note: This is one case where the idea of "recto" and "verso," or front
and back, is eliminated in terms of the rest of the description of the
map. This means that an ". . . on verso" note does not apply at all and
an "Includes . . ." note must contain data from one or both sides of the
sheet, whichever applies. The other case where this applies involves
two or more maps on both sides of a single sheet (see the particular
section in the following material).

MAP KEY

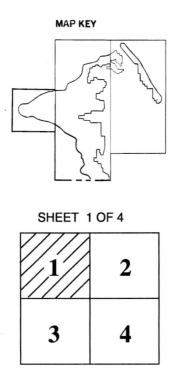

SHEET 1 OF 4

FIGURE 13.3. Map Keys to Indicate How Separate Maps Join

One Map on One Side of Multiple Sheets

Often when a map producer wishes to show an area, such as a moderate or large city or even a small country, at a large to very large scale, e.g., 1:25,000 or 1:50,000, because much detail needs to be shown, sections of the map will appear on separate sheets of paper (see Figure 13.4). Most usually this ends up being a single map on two or four sheets of paper. One of two things, and sometimes both, will tip off the cataloger to this situation and show that this is one map on several sheets as opposed to several individual maps: the border or neat line is not continuous on each sheet, so that it takes putting the multiple sheets together to see a complete border or neat line, and the title may start on one sheet and finish on one or more of the other sheets. In such a circumstance, it is necessary to be explicit at the beginning of the physical description as to how many sheets are involved, as opposed to adding sheet size as part of the given dimen-

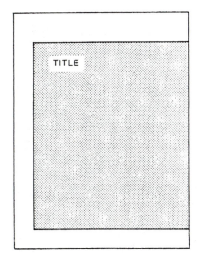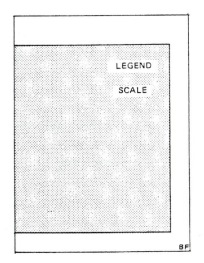

1 map on 2 sheets . . . *(Physical description)*

FIGURE 13.4. One Map on Two Sheets (*Source:*Reproduced from *Cartographic Materials: A Manual of Interpretation for the AACR2,* 1982, p. 87. Permission granted by the American Library Association.)

sions at the end of the physical description. Therefore, the physical description statement will begin:

300   1 map on 4 sheets : |b col. . . .

Two or More Maps on One Side of a Single Sheet

On occasion a group of maps is printed on one side of a single sheet, with each map related to the others through a particular topic. In such cases, the maps involved are known as "component" maps, each of which stands by itself cartographically but both or all of which are brought together on the single sheet; therefore, they are components of a larger whole (see Figure 13.5). Describe these in the following manner:

300   2 maps on 1 sheet . . .
300   4 maps on 1 sheet . . .

Two or More Maps on Both Sides of a Single Sheet

What should we do when there are two or more main maps printed on both sides of one sheet? This is nearly identical to the "one map that carries over" case, except that now we are talking about two separate maps (or more), as opposed to a single map that continues on to the other side of the sheet. In addition, each map is known as a "component" map, as in the previous case, because each could stand alone bibliographically and each fits the definition of a main map. Therefore, the beginning of the physical description is nearly the same as the carries-over case, but the difference is in identifying the number of main maps involved.

300   2 maps on 1 sheet : |b both sides . . .
300   3 maps on 1 sheet : |b both sides . . .

The cataloger can further clarify the actual layout in a note, explaining a circumstance such as having one map on one side and two on the opposite side of the sheet. Also, as stated earlier, the concept of "recto" and "verso" is nullified in the carries-over case.

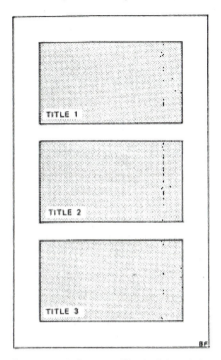

3 maps on 1 sheet . . . *(Physical description)*
Components: . . . *(Note area, 7B18)*

FIGURE 13.5. Three Maps on One Side of One Sheet (*Source:* Reproduced from *Cartographic Materials: A Manual of Interpretation for the AACR2,* 1982, p. 87. Permission granted by the American Library Association.)

Two or More Maps on Two or More Sheets

As mentioned at the start of this chapter, describing the situation of having multiple maps on two or more sheets becomes somewhat more complex. Under this circumstance we now have what is considered either a "map series" or a "collection" (see Figure 13.6). Map series and collections are the most common category of sheet maps, as denoted by Parker (1999): "Map series form the bulk of most map collections and the bibliographic control of the series as a whole and of its various parts is extremely important." Describing more than one map on more than one sheet is glossed over in the very last sentence

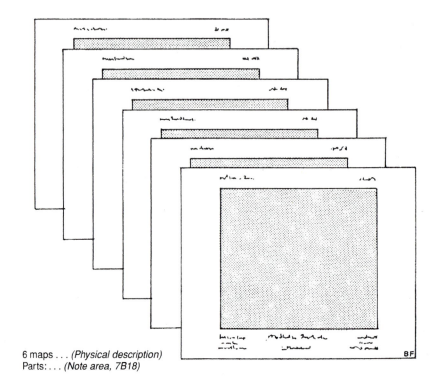

6 maps . . . *(Physical description)*
Parts: . . . *(Note area, 7B18)*

FIGURE 13.6. A Map Series (*Source:* Reproduced from *Cartographic Materials: A Manual of Interpretation for the AACR2,* 1982, p. 88. Permission granted by the American Library Association.)

as a part of Rule 3.5B2 in AACR2R, but it is much better explained in *Cartographic Materials,* in Rule 5D1k and its APPLICATION.

Application for a Completed Map Series or Collection

Whenever we have to describe a map series or collection that is a completed publication, we specify the number of maps unless they are too numerous to do so easily (see the third paragraph under Rule 3.5B1). This follows Rule 3.5B2, last paragraph, in AACR2R: "If an item consists of a number of sheets each of which is a complete map, etc., treat it as a collection and describe it as instructed in 3.5B1."

Turning to 3.5B1, we read, "Give the extent of a cartographic item. . . . In the case of other cartographic items, give the number of maps, etc." Since the number of maps counted would equal the number of sheets, it is not necessary to state explicitly ". . . on X sheets" in this case:

300   120 maps : |b col. ; |c each 48 x 45 cm.

However, one exception to not adding the number of sheets is when the maps outnumber the sheets, e.g., one map was printed on both sides of some of the sheets in the collection. Naturally, to be clear about this particularly rare situation, specify the number of sheets involved. Using the previous example, it would therefore read "120 maps on 116 sheets . . ." if two of the sheets each contained two maps.

Application When the Map Series or Collection Is Incomplete

An incomplete map series or collection is denoted by *not* specifying the number of maps involved, for obvious reasons; instead the Extent of item area simply says "maps." This is the opposite of having more than one map on a *single* sheet; in which case we specify the number of maps and give the phrase ". . . on 1 sheet" so that the situation is explicit.

300   maps ; |c 55 x 45 cm. or smaller.

This particular situation is not covered in the rules in AACR2R, so one must rely on the indispensable *Cartographic Materials* to discover its interpretation. CM's Rule 5B28 states, "In describing a multipart item that is not yet complete, give the specific material designation alone preceded by at least three spaces." The phrase "multipart item" harkens back to the earlier definition of "part," so don't be alarmed by the change in terminology; simply think of the reality of the ubiquitous U.S. Geological Survey's 7.5-minute series, and you will find that "multipart item" is an apt description. Be aware that the instruction of "preceded by at least three spaces" was written at a time when bibliographic records were still being done by hand on catalog cards. Many, if not all, of today's online systems will not allow three spaces to be retained in the field. Finally, the *Option* to Rule

5B28 notes that once the series or collection is completed, you may add the number of maps to the record.

OTHER PHYSICAL DETAILS
(FIELD 300, SUBFIELD "b")

Before proceeding with specifics relating to information that goes into subfield "b" of the 300 field, let's examine "recto" and "verso," when the concept does and does not apply, and how this concept impacts other areas of the bibliographic record. "Recto" and "verso," in other words "front" and "back," determine whether the common phrase "both sides" is employed within this subfield area.

The Concept and Application of "Recto" and "Verso"

If an item has one or more main maps on one side of the physical sheet, the item is considered to have a front, or "recto," and back, or "verso." This is important to understand because when giving the dimensions in subfield "c" of the 300 field, it is not necessary to give the dimensions of the sheet itself (although you may do so as an option) under this circumstance. Also, in terms of the list of general notes given in the record, the "Includes . . ." note will describe items found only on the recto, while the ". . . on verso" note will describe those items found only on the verso of the item. Put another way, the "Includes . . ." note lists other significant information included with the map(s) on the recto side, while the ". . . on verso" note completes the description of other significant information found on the side of the sheet that does not include the map(s) involved.

Once the cataloger has to supply the phrase "both sides," the concept of "recto" and "verso" is no longer valid. This means that in circumstances involving one or more main maps on each side of the sheet, or when the main map begins on one side of the sheet and is completed on the opposite side, the idea of the item having a front and back is not valid. In the next seciton you will find more specific information and examples of applying "both sides." However, let's also complete the corollary given in the previous paragraph regarding the need to provide the sheet size when "both sides" is applicable and also consider the impact of using the "Includes . . ." and ". . . on verso" notes. Since using "both sides" removes the concept of recto and verso, it becomes necessary to detail further the layout of the item by explicitly providing the sheet size in addition to the sizes for the maps involved. Likewise, as one might guess, the ". . . on verso" note no longer applies, and any further descriptive information is delineated using only the "Includes . . ." note. (Feel free to use multiple notes tied to the specific maps involved to describe more clearly a piece of information, such as an index, and the map that it relates to, as well as, or in place of, the "Includes . . ." note.)

Specifics of What Goes into 300 |b

Subfield "b" of the 300 field allows the cataloger to provide information about the physical arrangement and production aspects of the map. The Extent of item area (300, subfield "a") discussed earlier contains one of the components of this "b" subfield, that is, the layout of the map when it extends from one side of the sheet to the back or when multiple maps are printed on both sides of the sheet (see examples in the previous section as well).

```
300    1 map : |b col. ; |c . . .
300    1 map : |b both sides ; |c . . .
300    1 map : |b both sides, col. ; |c . . .
300    2 maps on 1 sheet : |b both sides, 1 col. ; |c . . .
```

Next comes the notation for indicating that the map is printed using more than one color, or the "col." designation. If there are multiple maps and only one or some of the entire group are printed using more than one color, this can also be specified, either by counting and including the number of colored maps or using the phrase "some col." if a small group of a large number of maps is involved or "most col." if the majority of maps in a large group are colored.

The meaning of "colored" in regard to maps is not clearly defined in Rule 3.5C5 of AACR2R. That is to say that the term "col." as used in 300 subfield "b" has a very specific meaning that must be understood in order to apply it correctly in the description. The APPLICATION to Rule 5C3 in CM does touch on this meaning:

> Monochromatic items are not considered colored regardless of
> the color of the ink or paper used. If the color of ink used on

monochromatic items is other than black, or if the paper is other than white, this may be recorded in a note.

The LC *Map Cataloging Manual* is more succinct and direct in this matter: "Monochromatic (i.e., having one color) items are not considered colored regardless of the color of ink or the paper used" (p. 2.14). For example, "Raisz maps" (pronounced "Royce"), a well-known genre of maps, were often printed in brown ink. These maps would *not* be given the term "col." in subfield "b" according to the rule interpretations noted here; instead, a note such as "Printed in brown ink" would be added to the record.

```
300   1 map : |b col. . . .
300   4 maps on 1 sheet : |b 2 col. . . .
300   2 maps on 1 sheet : |b both sides, 1 col. . . .
300      maps : |b some col. ; |c . . .
300      maps : |b most col. ; |c . . .
```

In addition, if the map has been mechanically reproduced, as in the case of xerographic (commonly known as Xerox) copies or diazo (blue-line or black-line) prints, one needs to indicate this here by providing the term "photocopy" or "photocopies," if more than one map is involved. Alternately, specify the method of production or reproduction in subfield "b" using the generic name of the process, e.g., blue-line or computer printout, according to Rule 3.5C3. Specify the mechanical production method in a general note whenever "photocopy" is used.

```
300   1 map : |b photocopy ; |c . . .
300   2 maps on 1 sheet : |b photocopies ; |c . . .
500   Blue-line print.
300   1 map : |b blue-line; |c . . .
300   1 map : |b computer printout, co.; |c . . .
```

The last kind of information given in this subfield has to do with the methodology for mounting the map, such as whether a paper map was glued to a cloth backing or attached to rollers so that it can be hung and then unrolled for use.

300   1 map : |b col., mounted on cloth ; |c . . .
300   1 map : |b col., mounted on wooden rollers ; |c . . .
300   1 map : |b mounted on cloth and plastic rollers ; |c . . .

Application of "Back to Back" versus "Both Sides"

In the vast majority of cases, the cataloger will be describing the situation of maps, or portions of a single map, appearing on both sides of the sheet by using the phrase "both sides" in subfield "b". However, in one specific circumstance, even though a main map does appear on each side of the sheet, the phrase "back to back" must be applied (in French, *tête-bêche*). In *Cartographic Materials,* Rule 5D1j states, "If the cartographic item has maps printed on both sides, one of which is a *translation* of the other, record the dimensions of the map. Add the sheet size, if considered necessary," and the example given shows the use of "back to back" in this situation. The key point is that one map must be a translation of the other; needless to say, this is a fairly rare occurrence, except for maps produced in bilingual countries such as Canada.

300   2 maps on 1 sheet : |b back to back, col. ; |c . . .

DIMENSIONS (FIELD 300, SUBFIELD "c")

Rule 3.5D1 in AACR2R tells us that a cartographic item must be measured both in terms of height and width and to give these dimensions in centimeters. At this point the infamous line "measured within the neat lines" appears in Rule 3.5D1 and "measured between the neat lines" in Rule 5D1b in *Cartographic Materials.* This is the concept that gives the new map cataloger the chills and makes him or her ask, "What is a neat line?" Quoting from the APPLICATION following Rule 5D1b in *Cartographic Materials,* "The neat line is a line which encloses the detail of a map. There is only one neat line on a map. . . . If there is no neat line, measure the maximum extent of the cartographic detail." While indeed there is only one neat line on a map, at times multiple lines, or boxes if you will, one inside the other, are found on the map, and other times portions of lines enclose two or more sides of the map (see Figure 13.7). Another circumstance that allows you to measure a kind of box around the map is when text and/or illustrations frame the map, leaving an easily identifiable outline from which to take the measurements.

If only one line surrounds the map, it obviously is the neat line, but what are the other lines, actually the areas created between the sets of lines, called? If two sets of lines are printed on the map, one within the other, the neat line is the innermost line and the one that is closest to the geographic detail; the next line frames the neat line, and the space between is called the border; therefore, the outer line is the border line. If a third line frames the two inner lines and map, the space from that third line to the outside edge of the sheet is called the margin. An excellent illustration of this is shown in Figure 13.7.

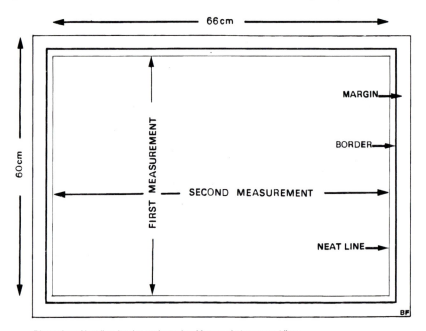

Dimensions. Neat line, border, and margins. Measure between neat lines
1 map : col. ; 60 x 66 cm

FIGURE 13.7. Neat Line Measurements (*Source:* Reproduced from *Cartographic Materials: A Manual of Interpretation for the AACR2,* 1982, p. 108. Permission granted by the American Library Association.)

Reading Position and Its Impact on Measuring Dimensions

Pay attention also to the way the map is laid out because the dimensional measurements should be taken when the map is in its "reading position" (see Figure 13.8). The APPLICATION to Rule 5D1a in *Cartographic Materials* states, "When the map is placed in reading position, 'height' is the top-to-bottom measurement of the map; 'width' is the left-right measurement of the map."

The cataloger must take the height and width measurements from the neat line when it is available, and the order in which they are given is height first and width second. Following from the previous "reading position" statement, the first measurement taken is from top to bottom, and the second measurement, from left to right. Therefore, in the case of one map on one side of the sheet, the "on one sheet" is implied, and this makes giving a sheet size unnecessary in the dimensions area. An example of this situation would be:

1 map : |b col. ; |c 24 x 36 cm.

Not:

1 map : |b col. ; |c 24 x 36 cm., on sheet 30 x 40 cm.

If a neat line is not printed on the map, then give the height and width of the geographic extent of the map itself and include the sheet size:

1 map : |b col. ; |c 24 x 36 cm., on sheet 28 x 40 cm.

Once again, if we have a single map in sections, or if a single map continues onto the opposite side of the sheet, or if we move from one map to multiple maps, the circumstances change; it becomes necessary to be explicit and to give the sheet size along with the size of the map or maps involved, as is detailed more explicitly in the following.

When to Give the Sheet Size

Why do we have to give yet one more set of dimensions, in this case the size of the physical sheets of paper that the map(s) is (are)

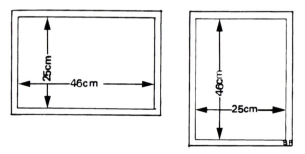

Dimensions. Two sizes of map in a series
; 25 x 46 cm and 46 x 25 cm

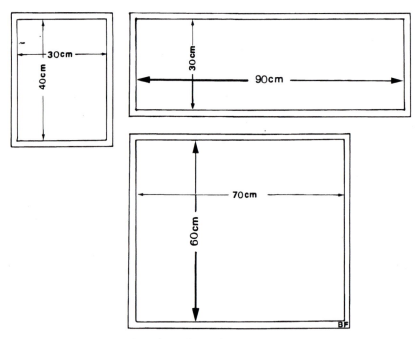

Dimensions. More than two sizes of maps in a series
; 60 x 90 cm or smaller

FIGURE 13.8. Map Sheets Showing Differing Reading Positions (*Source:* Reproduced from *Cartographic Materials: A Manual of Interpretation for the AACR2,* 1982, p. 121. Permission granted by the American Library Association.)

printed on, when we are already providing the size of the map(s) involved? First, it does give the user a general understanding of the overall size of the physical item, which can be helpful in terms of making choices between similar titles. Second, this set of dimensions may assist with internal map filing decisions when different types of drawers are available for map storage. Last, sometimes the dimensions for the map itself cannot be determined or cannot be determined easily; therefore, the dimensions for the sheet provide an understanding of overall size.

The following circumstances meet the criteria for giving the sheet size in the dimensions statement:

> A single map in sections or segments
> A single map that starts on one side of the sheet and finishes on the other side
> A single map on multiple sheets
> A single map that is less than one-half of one of the dimensions of the sheet or has substantial additional information, such as a large amount of text
> Two or more maps on a single sheet
> Two or more maps on multiple sheets
> Whenever a single map or a single map in sections/segments is so irregularly shaped that it is difficult to determine the size of the map itself (In this case, give only the sheet size.) For example:

> 300   1 map : |b col. ; |c on sheet 50 x 70 cm.

Optionally, the cataloger may give the sheet size in any circumstance; however, one will quickly understand that with a single map on one side of a single sheet, this is unnecessary information in terms of understanding the overall layout of the map.

Measuring a Circular or Oval-Shaped Map

What does one do with a map that is circular or oval in shape? Rule 5D1e of *Cartographic Materials* explains this precisely: "Give the diameter of a circular map, etc. and specify it as such." For example:

> 1 map : |b col. ; |c 30 cm. in diam., on sheet 38 x 42 cm.

A Map Cut into Parts After Its Issuance

Sometimes it may be necessary for a map library to physically alter a map by cutting it into two or more sizes, such as when the map is too large for a standard map cabinet drawer or when preservation means, such as encapsulation, are needed to extend the life of the map involved. In such cases, how do we give the measurements? The APPLICATION to Rule 5B2a of *Cartographic Materials* explains that we should "[d]escribe the physical state of the item in hand at the time of cataloging regardless of how it was issued by the publisher/printer, e.g., if an item was originally issued on one sheet but subsequently dissected, it is described in its dissected form." It would, however, be worthwhile to other catalogers to provide a note detailing the item as it existed at the time of publication, if that can be readily determined:

> 1 map : |b col., dissected in 2 pieces . . .
> *Note:* Originally published on one sheet.

"Bleeding Edge" and How to Determine Dimensions in This Case

Yes, the term "bleeding edge" does sound rather dangerous, and those of us who work with maps sometimes end up with bleeding paper cuts, but this is actually a technical term that the cataloger must know. "Bleeding edge" literally means that the geographic detail on the map extends to the edge of the sheet that it is printed on in one or more directions (see Figure 13.9). To be even more explicit, the geographic detail bleeds along the entire length of the edge of the sheet, not just a small portion of the edge (see the following section for an explanation of this different situation). My apologies for sounding so gruesome, but it is important to understand this phenomenon in relation to how we normally take a measurement, that is to say, as opposed to measuring from a neat line. Rule 3.5D1 in AACR2R does touch on this particular circumstance: "or if it bleeds off the edge, give the greater or greatest dimensions of the map itself." A more explicit explanation is given in the APPLICATION to Rule 5D1d in *Cartographic Materials,* which states that the "greatest dimensions" are the extent of the cartographic coverage on the map. Therefore, if the map bleeds to the edge in any direction, and most usually the printing process causes the map to bleed in either two or all four directions,

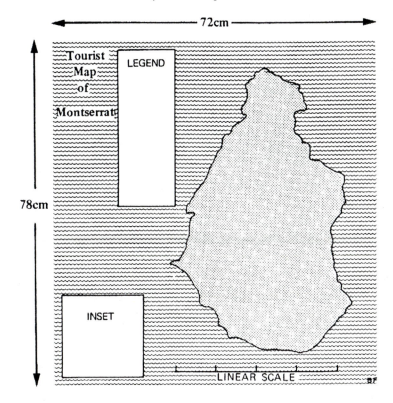

Dimensions. Bleeding edge
1 map : col. ; 78 x 72 cm

FIGURE 13.9. Bleeding Edge Map Dimensions (*Source:* Reproduced by *Cartographic Materials: A Manual of Interpretation for the AACR2,* 1982, p. 113. Permission granted by the American Library Association.)

measure from the edge of the map sheet to the opposite neat line or opposite edge of the map sheet and give the resulting dimensions.

What to Do When a Portion of the Geographic Detail Extends Beyond the Neat Line

In a similar phenomenon to the "bleeding edge" situation just described, sometimes a map will have a portion of its geographic detail carry over or break through the neat line in one or more directions. The primary difference between this scenario and a bleeding edge is that it occurs along only a portion of one or more sides of the sheet. In addition, the geographic detail may or may not extend completely to the edge of the sheet. Once again, this causes some consternation in terms of the correct way to determine dimensions for the map in question. Following the "greatest dimensions" line of thinking, measure from the point where the geographic detail stops to the opposite neat line or to the opposite edge of the geographic detail, if it also carries over the neat line in the opposing direction. Give the resulting dimension(s).

Two or More Maps on Multiple Sheets

What do we do if we have a collection or map series in terms of measuring dimensions? And, perhaps more perplexing, what do you do if some of the maps and/or some of the sheets are of different sizes? First, keep in mind that whenever you are providing dimensions for more than one map on multiple sheets, this fits the criteria for providing the sheet size(s) as well as the map size(s). Let's look at the two parts, the maps themselves and the sheets they are printed on, separately.

When "Component" Maps, Maps in a Series or in a Collection, Are the Same Size

If all of the component maps, or maps in a series or collection, are of the same size, indicate this by adding the word "each" in front of the given dimensions. This clearly imparts to the reader that all of the maps are of the same size. For instance:

    300   2 maps on 1 sheet : |b both sides ; |c each 40 x 45 cm.,
           sheet 45 x 50 cm.
    300   maps : |b col. ; |c each 50 x 30 cm., on sheets 55 x 35 cm.

If the sheet sizes are of two different sizes for all of them, give both sets of dimensions. If they are of three or more sizes in either dimension, give the greatest height and greatest width of the dimensions for all of the sheets, followed by the phrase "or smaller." For example:

    300   maps : |b col. ; |c each 50 x 30 cm., on sheets 55 x 35 cm.
           and 52 x 37 cm.
    300   maps : |b col. ; |c each 50 x 30 cm., on sheets 60 x 40 cm.
           or smaller.

Note: If you use the word "on" in subfield "a" as in the first example in this subsection, then do not repeat it in subfield "c". And, you must supply the word "on" in subfield "c" if it is not supplied at the beginning of the physical description statement as shown in the second, third, and fourth examples.

When "Component" Maps, Maps in a Series or in a Collection, Are Not the Same Size

Rule 3.5D1, last paragraph, in AACR2R, and the matching Rule 5D1k in *Cartographic Materials,* specifies that "[i]f the maps, etc., in a collection are of two sizes, give both. If they are of more than two sizes, give the greatest height of any of them followed by the greatest width of any of them and the words *or smaller.*" Once again we see the "rule of three" in action in this part of the bibliographic description. Examples for both of these cases follow:

    300   2 maps on 1 sheet : |b col. ; |c 25 x 22 cm. and 18 x 20 cm.,
           sheet 30 x 30 cm.
    300   3 maps on 1 sheet : |b both sides, col. ; |c 28 x 27 cm.
           or smaller, sheet 30 x 30 cm.
    300   60 maps ; 44 x 55 cm. and 48 x 55 cm., on sheets
           50 x 58 cm.
    300   60 maps ; 60 x 70 cm. or smaller., on sheets 65 x 75 cm.

If the maps *and* the sheets are of three or more sizes, then employ the phrase "or smaller" after taking the greatest height and width of all of the maps and sheets after *both* sets of dimensions. For example:

    300   68 maps : |b col. ; |c 45 x 44 cm. or smaller, on sheets
           65 x 53 cm. or smaller.

Providing Folded Measurements

Whenever a map can be folded to show an outer panel, or into a cover of some type, provide the folded dimensions as the last part of the Dimensions area in the 300 field. This follows from Rule 3.5D1, sixth paragraph, in AACR2R or Rule 5D1h in *Cartographic Materials,* both of which state, "If a map, etc., is printed with an outer cover within which it is intended to be folded . . . give the sheet size in folded form as well as the size of the map, etc." Naturally, *Cartographic Materials* has an APPLICATION to explain further what is happening here and what to do under these circumstances:

> This rule refers to items which are designed to be folded but are available flat or folded. Base the measurements on the size of the panel, section, etc. This rule does not apply to items which may have been folded for convenience (e.g., by publisher, manufacturer, distributor, or subsequent owners) but have not been designed to be folded.

Allow me to reiterate a couple of these points and also to provide some guidance in how to word the folded measurements in field 300, subfield "c". First, note "within which it is *intended to be folded*" (my emphasis); a good rule of thumb for intent in the case of a panel is whether a complete title is shown when the map is folded. If this is the case, also hence the term "panel title," then the wording in the 300 field should be:

300   1 map : |b col. ; |c 58 x 68 cm., folded to 21 x 10 cm.

If, however, when you fold the map along its folding lines the title is "cut off" or not complete, it becomes obvious that the map was folded for convenience, as mentioned in the APPLICATION to Rule 5D1h, most usually so that it will fit into an envelope, plastic sleeve, or some other kind of container.

As for the nuance in wording, remember that if a map has a cover that it folds *into,* i.e., inside the outer cover, the wording changes to accommodate this fact ("folded to" versus "folded in"):

300   1 map : |b col. ; |c 58 x 68 cm., folded in cover 21 x 10 cm.

Also, it is possible to have a flat map with a panel printed on it, to which the "designed to be folded" portion of the APPLICATION refers. Quite simply, the publisher printed a run of several hundred or thousand of the maps involved and kept a small portion aside to be sold or distributed as flat maps, even though the panel is printed on the sheet; the remaining maps were eventually folded as designed and distributed in that manner.

Providing Measurements for a Container

The last set of dimensions that can be given, if needed, involves the container in which the map was distributed. Most often this applies to a map, and sometimes other accompanying material such as a text, distributed in an envelope. However, this also applies to any other kind of container, except a cover (remember that the map itself is attached to the cover that it is folded into). Other containers may include a box or tube.

Boxes and Tubes As Containers

Rule 3.5D5 in AACR2R notes that providing measurements for a container is optional, and in the case of a box or tube, most of the time it makes sense not to apply the option, since the map itself will be stored elsewhere. However, if you choose to provide the measurements of these types of containers, add them as the last part of the dimensions statement:

300   15 maps : |b col. ; |c each 75 x 48 cm., in box 40 x 20
        x 20 cm.
300   1 map : |b col. ; |c 103 x 89 cm., in tube 8 cm. in diam.

Note that in the case of the maps in a box, the folded size of the *maps* is not important, and therefore not given, similar to a map that is folded in a cover.

Envelope As Container

Oftentimes an envelope, serving as the container for the map, provides a handy way of storing and organizing maps on either standard library shelving or in a vertical file cabinet. Thus, it is useful to give the envelope size, even if the envelope might be discarded and the map stored flat in a map case. In fact, if the envelope provides a different title and/or statement of responsibility, and especially if a series or other type of number is found on the envelope but not on the map, it is strongly advised to give the envelope size, in part to justify information found elsewhere in the record and in part to assist other catalogers in the "Is this a match?" decision. Finally, we also give the envelope size because we are describing the item as the publisher issued it, and as other libraries received it, providing yet another element with which the cataloger can determine a matching bibliographic record:

300   1 map ; |c 68 x 70 cm., folded in envelope 31 x 23 cm.
        + |e legend sheet

Once again, the folded size of the map is not important because it resides within the envelope; therefore, the envelope size becomes the defining last dimension in this area.

Chapter 14

Notes in the Record

Catalogers typically provide a variety of notes in the bibliographic records for the materials they catalog as a way of sharing specific additional information with the users, and sheet maps are no exception. In fact, because of their nontextual graphic nature, maps and other types of media, such as photographs, videorecordings, and art prints, demand much more in the way of notes than monographs. Maps convey information primarily through a visual context, and by using symbols and sometimes color, they provide the cataloger with frequent opportunities to include notes that enhance the description of the item. Notes that further explain what the maps show in terms of geographic coverage, physical landscape (if it applies), and additional or accompanying textual information are important means of conveying information to patrons.

WHO BENEFITS FROM INCLUDING NOTES IN THE RECORD?

Why add multiple notes to a bibliographic record for maps, and who benefits from the cataloger's efforts? First and foremost, we add notes to benefit our patrons, to give them a better understanding beyond just the title, scale, and provided subject headings. What the map contains in the way of information, both cartographic and noncartographic, is useful to convey. For instance, to a patron who wants to hike or camp in a remote area, knowing the ruggedness of the local landscape and extent of elevation, otherwise known as "relief," in advance would be helpful; therefore, applying a "relief note" is useful to this patron. To another patron seeking knowledge about the changes to a particular town or city over time, including a note that says some textual history is a part of the map could be helpful to his or her research needs. Sometimes indicating what a map does *not* show can also be very valuable; thus, a "geographic coverage" note could help identify the fact that a country or state is not part of a particular map, thereby steering a patron to a different map.

Another group of individuals who benefit from notes in the bibliographic record are catalogers seeking to identify existing copy to use for their own libraries' collections. Notes such as where the title came from, additional comments regarding the physical aspects of the map not given in the 300 field, information about responsibility for the production and/or publication of the map, and, most important, notes for any kind of unique number(s) assist the next cataloger more than the patron.

Finally, it is normal for a map cataloger to provide notes that justify including a tracing for a person or corporate body that differs from the main entry heading. This assists other catalogers in understanding the reason for additional added entries in the record and can also assist the patron, or the reference staff helping the patron, in understanding the role that other individuals, companies, or agencies performed in creating the map.

ORDER AND "CATEGORIES" OF NOTES

AACR2R asks us to provide general notes in a specified order, as for all other types of materials, and very specific kinds of notes placed in 5XX fields other than the 500 most usually follow in numerical order; therefore, "Nature and scope of item" information would come before notes regarding the source of the title given or other title-related information. So, notes regarding the type of relief displayed, "Shows . . ." or "Also shows . . ." notes, and the important "Covers . . ." or "Geographic coverage . . ." note typically start the list of notes given in a bibliographic record for a map. These are followed by "Source of title" notes, such as "Panel title," and "Statements of responsibility" notes, such as "Geology compiled by . . ." A list of examples of actual notes, to assist in the sometimes-frustrating problem of how to formulate them, is given at the end of this chapter. In addition, Chapter 7 on the "Note area" in *Cartographic Materials* provides excellent examples under each note type, as well as helpful explanations on how they should be applied.

Within the list of notes for cartographic materials, however, it sometimes makes sense to start the list slightly out of the prescribed order because the importance of conveying particular information to our patrons outweighs the order promulgated in the rules. One such example is to provide a "Summary," or 520 note, ahead of those for "Nature and scope of item," and others, when the cataloger thinks that the title is so vague or misleading that this becomes a very important piece of information to provide at the earliest point in the record. Therefore, expect to find records that occasionally have notes out of order, but do try to follow the prescribed order of notes delineated in AACR2R as much as possible.

Finally, two categories of notes are listed here to help the cataloger decide what should be included in the record. The "essential" list provides notes that assist the map user in his or her decision to retrieve and use the map. The "additional" list contains notes that primarily assist other catalogers but could also be useful to the more savvy library patron.

Essential Notes
Relief method notes
Geographic coverage
Type of reproduction (e.g., blue-line print, Xerox copy, "Negative")
Source of title if not from within the neat lines of the map
Date of situation or inferred publication
Publication information
Orientation of the map (if other than north)
Additional mathematical information, including base map information
Other physical aspects (e.g., wall map, hand colored)
Contents (when more than one map on the sheet or for small map sets/series)
Unique numbering of any kind (always provide this note to help fellow catalogers)

Additional Information Notes
Other or additional statements of responsibility
"Insets:" or "Ancillary maps:" note (listing by title)
Index information

Accompanying material (if not given in the 300 |e subfield)
"Includes" note
"On verso" note
Languages (use the 546 field to bring out the circumstances re-
   lating to other languages on the item, such as a legend that is
   given in two or more languages)

NOTES TO JUSTIFY PROVIDING
ADDED ENTRIES

The APPLICATION to Rule 1F2 in *Cartographic Materials* specifies
the reason for justifying an added entry for a cartographic publisher
in this manner: "If it is known that the publisher is responsible for the
work[8] but there is no statement of responsibility on the item, a note
(7B6) may be made to indicate that the publisher is also responsible
for its preparation."

Going forward to Rule 7B6 in CM, which is the area for notes on
statements of responsibility, we find these instructions:

> Make notes on variant names of persons or bodies named in
> statements of responsibility if these are considered to be impor-
> tant for identification. Give statements of responsibility not re-
> corded in the title and statement of responsibility area. Make
> notes on persons or bodies connected with a work, or significant
> persons or bodies connected with previous editions, not already
> named in the description.

Two parts of this rule are quite significant in terms of considering a
cartographic publisher as an added entry. These are "if these are considered to be important for identification" and "Make notes on persons or bodies connected with a work . . . not already named in the description." While this asks only that the cataloger make notes for
persons or bodies associated with the production of the map that are
not named in a formal statement of responsibility, the extension can
be made that a known cartographic publisher usually has a role in the
production of the map and thus can be "considered to be important
for identification" and should be traced.

Footnote 8 in Rule 1F2 states, "This knowledge depends on the cataloguer's familiarity with the field and with the preparation and publishing practices of the body concerned. If in doubt, do not make a note."

EXAMPLES OF NOTES

Note: Most of the following are based on or taken from Salinger and Zagon's (1984) *Notes for Catalogers: A Sourcebook for Use with AACRZ* .

- *Nature and scope of the item*

    Shows . . .
    Also shows . . .
    Geographic coverage complete in . . .
    Relief shown by contours and spot heights. Depths shown by isolines and soundings.
    Perspective map.
    Cadastral map.

- *Source of title proper*

    Envelope title.
    Panel title.
    Cover title.
    Title from publisher's catalog.

- *Variations in title*

    Collective title of village maps: A guide to the villages of Wayne County.
    In upper margin: Old roads from Griffith's map 1794.

- *Parallel titles and other title information*

    At head of title: . . .
    Each sheet individually titled.
    Stamped on: Census map.

- *Statements of responsibility*

    "Designed by . . ."
    "Aerial photography flown by . . ."
    "Copyright . . ."
    "Base map prepared by the U.S. Geological Survey in coop-
        eration with the Soil Conservation Service."
    "Lithographed by DMAAC 1-79."

- *Edition and history*

    Facsimile.
    A later state of the map first published in . . .
    Taken from . . .
    Includes various issues of some sheets.
    Originally printed on 2 sheets, each 117 x 88 cm.

- *Mathematical and other cartographic data*

    Prime meridian: Ferro and Paris.
    Oriented with north to the upper right.
    Vertical profiles: Horizontal scale ca. 1:3,500,000, vertical
        scale ca. 1:10,000.
    Military grid.

- *Publication, distribution, etc.*

    Printed in Singapore by Singapore Offset Printing Pte. Ltd.
    Distributed by Grosset & Dunlap.
    "Mex. D.F. Abril 1951."

- *Physical description*

    Wall map with metal grommets for hanging.
    Blue-line print.
    Hand colored.
    Watermark: C. and I. Honig.
    Designed to be folded to 23 x 11 cm.

- *Accompanying material*

  Accompanied by index map: Index / the Maryland National
  Capital Park and Planning Commission (1 leaf : photo-
  copy; 86 x 106 cm.)
  Accompanies . . .
  Plastic index device in pocket.

- *Series*

  Not all sheets have series designation on them.
  Series title from distributor's catalog.
  Two sheets have series designation: Glacier map series.

- *Contents*

  Indexed for selected buildings.
  Insets: . . .
  Ancillary maps: . . .
  Includes notes, text, location map, and col. ill.
  Hiking information, camping regulations, text, trails index,
  and col. ill. on verso.
  Bibliography in text: p. 12.
  Contents: Area 1. Lake Mead area – Area 2. Hoover Dam-
  Lake Mohave – Area 3. Lake Mohave-Needles – Area 4.
  Needles-Lake Havasu.

- *Numbers*

  "Base 881369 (R46079) 7-97."
  Publisher's No.: 247.
  In lower right corner: JFK/79-81.
  "U.Ed. 80-488."
  "*GPO: 1994—301-085/80171 Reprint 1986."

- *Copy being described and library's holdings* (for local records
  only)

  Library's copy lacking sheet 10.
  Library's copy missing lower right corner and encapsulated.
  E & MS Library copy in envelope (31 x 23 cm.)

SECTION IV:
OTHER ACCESS POINTS

Chapter 15

Classification Using the LC G-Schedule

Although the Library of Congress (LC) classification system certainly is not the only one available for institutions to use for organizing their map collections, it is the one most widely used in North America, if not the world at large. The strength of this classification scheme is that it arranges and subarranges geographic areas of the world in a straightforward and meaningful way. In addition, through the use of what are generically called "subject cutters," although these are not technically cutters and will be referred to as subject "codes," this system also provides for a means of subarranging maps of the same geographic area by topic, putting those maps of the same area and with the same topic, e.g., of a county or state in the United States that shows the geology of the area, together, but then arranged chronologically, and, if necessary, by author.

COMPONENTS OF THE LIBRARY OF CONGRESS CALL NUMBER

A geography classification, or G-class, LC call number consists of up to seven components. The more complex and/or detailed the map is in terms of level of geographic area, topical nature, and physical layout, and whether the map is an original or a reproduction, the more components there are to the call number itself. The individual components include the following:

G	= Classification letter
4282	= Classification number from the G-Schedule
.M59	= Geographic area cutter
C5	= Subject area cutter
1935	= Date of situation (or scale, e.g., "s10" for a set)
.G4	= Author cutter

Also, if the map is a reproduction, then an additional year, e.g., 1995, is added as the last component of the call number for the date the map was reproduced. In "string" form the elements of this call number would be written or typed as follows:

G4282.M59C5 1935 |b .G4 [reproduction year if necessary]

Spacing conventions in the call number, as specified in Chapter 1, "Classification," in the LC *Map Cataloging Manual,* are that "[a] space [be] inserted immediately preceding and immediately following the date/scale information. A space is also inserted immediately preceding any filing location [author cutter] information" (p. 1.1). The subfield tag of "b" in the call number string is shown in its location for the purposes of convention in using the MARC 21 standard; note that if it were withdrawn from the call number, the spacing standard would follow that outlined by LC.

The "G" in the Call Number

Quite simply, this represents LC classification Schedule "G" for "Geography, Maps, Anthropology, [and] Recreation," as opposed to any of the other forty-four schedules for disciplines, such as class "Q" for "Science."

Classification Number

The four-digit classification number comes from the highly detailed list provided in the LC G-Schedule. For atlases, the class number range is G1000-3122 (see Box 15.1). For sheet maps, the class number range is from G3180-9980; "3180" represents celestial maps while 9980 represents "Maps of unidentified places." In between these two extremes, the Earth is represented by class numbers from its largest form, G3200 for maps of the world, to more refined divisions of the world that range from the two hemispheres to continents to countries and so forth. What makes this classification arrangement a true geographic arrangement "system" is the changing of the fourth digit in the number to mean something very specific, such as 0 (zero) or 5 meaning "general" and 1 or 6 meaning that the map is topical in nature. Once the fourth digit is changed to a 2, 3, or 4 (or their companion numbers of 7, 8, and 9), a geographic area cutter must also be

---

BOX 15.1. Atlas Treatment

The G classification schedule includes a separate set of numbers for atlases. These numbers range from G1000 through G3122. The list for atlases contains fewer numbers and therefore is less flexible than the classification numbers for maps. For instance, it is much easier to find a number for an individual island in an archipelago by using the map numbers than by using the atlas numbers. However, one uses the same geographic area cutters and the same table of subject cutters for atlases as for maps.

---

given because each of these numbers means that the map is of a region; political subunit, such as a county; or a city. For more detail follow the discussion in the section Creating a Library of Congress Call Number. And, naturally, use the "Special Instructions and Tables of Subdivisions for Atlases and Maps" found on pages 206 to 211 in the 1976 edition of the LC G-Schedule, and the "Classification" chapter in the LC *Map Cataloging Manual,* to further your learning and understanding of the principles involved in this classification scheme. (Unfortunately, the 2001 edition of the LC G-Schedule does not contain the instructions for creating a call number. However, the instructions have been updated and are available online at <http://lcweb.loc. gov/catdir/cpso/class_g.html>.)

Geographic Area Cutter

The geographic area cutter is an alphanumeric designation for specific local places at the regional (or natural feature), political (county, state, province, etc., if one of these types has not been assigned its own classification number), and city levels. The database of these cutters is ever growing as new places are mapped and cutters for them are assigned.

The table itself is first divided at the classification level for a place, and then, within each classification number, the geographic area cutters are listed in alphanumeric order. The list of cutters can be understood only in context with the classification number for a specific geographic area because the same alphanumeric cutter can mean the same thing in many different places, e.g., .C6 means "Coasts" for those states in the United States which have a coastline along an ocean, sea, or lake, or it can mean many different places if not linked to its larger political entity, e.g., .P5 means "Philadelphia" in the state of Pennsylvania but "Perry" in the state of Georgia. Therefore, as mentioned in the previous discussion, if the last digit is a 2, 3, 4, 7, 8, or 9, then one must turn to the geographic area cutter tables to determine specifically what number to assign as the representative for the region, political division, or city displayed on the map. The bottom line is that each region, political unit, and city within a country or state has a unique cutter to represent it in the call number.

Only one geographic area cutter may be assigned to a call number; therefore, in the case where either one map shows multiple geographic areas or multiple maps of more than one geographic area (remember the discussion on "component" maps in Chapter 13) are being cataloged, additional geographic area cutters are given in one or more 052 fields.

In 2001 the Library of Congress launched its new Web site for online access to the entire LC classification system, the *Library of Congress Classification Web,* distributed by LC's Cataloging Distribution Service. Here, in one place, are all of the classification schedules, but, more important, for those cataloging maps, it was the first time a link to geographic cutters on a worldwide basis was provided. Then, in late 2001, the "Electronic G" schedule was made available in the *Classification Plus* software, which is easier to use because it is specific to the G-Schedule and links directly to the geographic cutters database. The geographic cutters database contains nearly 110,000 individual cutters for places and continues to grow daily.

The problem with the microfiche list of geographic cutters for places in the United States, launched in 1989 as *Geographic Cutters* by the LC's Geography and Map Division, was that its internal list of cutters for places worldwide had been growing rapidly, but catalogers outside of LC did not have access to this database of information. The "Electronic G" and the *Classification Web* is a godsend for finding geographic cutters for places outside of the United States; it means that catalogers everywhere do not have to attempt to find specific cutters, either by locating LC copy for bibliographic records in OCLC's WorldCat or directly through their online catalog.

Subject Area Code

The subject area code, generically referred to as the "subject cutter," is very similar in nature to the geographic area cutter in terms of its attempt to identify unique, specific topics within a broader scheme. Table IV, "Subject Subdivisions," in the G-Schedule lists subject codes within each of seventeen topical areas or disciplines.

The topical areas run from the letters "A" to "S" but do not include the letters "I" and "O," presumably so that if a new discipline arises in the future and needs its own designation, the Library of Congress can expand the list using one or both of these letters. Each letter represents a topical area; for example, the letter "A" is used for maps and atlases of "Special categories," such as Index maps and remote-sensing images, and the letter "C" represents categories of "Physical science" maps, such as geology and meteorology. Within each lettered area specific subdisciplines are given individual alphanumeric designations so that they represent a map of that particular subdiscipline, and these alphanumeric designations are the subject cutters. Examples of very commonly used subject cutters are .C2 for topographic maps, .C5 for maps of the geology of a specific area, and .P2 for road maps.

Subject codes *must* be assigned whenever the last digit in the classification number is a 1 or 6 because these two fourth digits mean "this is a subject-based map." Subject codes *may* be assigned, and always after the geographic area cutter, to those maps whose classification number ends with a 2, 3, or 4 or their partner digits of 7, 8, or 9. I specified *may* be assigned in this circumstance because a map of a region, political entity, or city can either be general in nature or created to show a specific topic, such as the subway system in a city.

The most difficult part of assigning the subject code is when a map has, or might be determined to have, multiple topics involved, in which case the cataloger must determine if one of the topics takes precedence over the other(s). At times, this simply cannot be determined based on the information given in the map or by what the map actually shows, in which case cataloger's judgment comes into play, and he or she may choose a primary topic based on local collection needs or other factors.

However, since classification and subject analysis are inextricably linked, following the discussion on subject analysis found in Chapter 4, "Access," in the LC *Map Cataloging Manual*, helps tremendously in the thought process for assigning both a subject code and a primary subject heading for a map. In fact, the following statement in Chapter 1, "Classification," in the manual clearly states this case:

"Subject Cutters are assigned to materials according to the general guidelines for subject analysis" (p. 1.8).

In addition, the manual specifically states that in order to determine the primary subject or topic of a given map,

> [s]ubject analysis is based on what an item is as opposed to what it says it is. However, try not to defy the author or publisher in assessing the purpose of the publication. For materials where judgment of subject content is especially difficult, give publisher's intent special emphasis in classification. (p. 4.2)

Sometimes the "on what an item is as opposed to what it says it is" can be a very fine line, but one should err on the side of what the map is about in these cases. Second, "publisher's intent" is most readily determined by the title or titles for the map(s), although sometimes this is in conflict with what the map shows. The cataloger is instructed in such cases that "[i]f the author's or publisher's statement of purpose or contents of an item is actually misleading, the statement of content (title, etc.) may be ignored, and the work classed without regard to the stated publisher's intent." Fortunately, the majority of maps have titles that accurately represent the intent of the map, and the chore of assigning both a subject code and a primary subject heading is not that difficult.

Finally, although this has not been mentioned previously, only one subject code may be assigned to a call number, meaning that either a primary topic is determined and the subject code is based upon it or a primary topic is assigned by the cataloger and then the code is given. Additional subject codes can be given in one or more 072 fields in the record, if the cataloger chooses to provide them.

Date of Situation

The "date of situation," or the date used in the call number, was first mentioned briefly in Chapter 12, "Publication Information," as part of a discussion contrasting publication date and date of situation. As noted in that chapter, often the publication date is used as the date of situation simply because no information is provided that details when the cartographic information was created for the item. It is very important to attempt to provide a date of situation for a sheet map because, once again, the cartographic information is the key component to any map, and providing knowledge as to how recent that information happens to be is often critical to the map user.

The best resource on explaining date of situation is the LC *Map Cataloging Manual,* in the unit "Date of Situation" (pp. 1.16-1.18). This unit includes detailed examples for a variety of situations; a general set is reproduced here:

Title:	*Master plan, population in 2000.*
Date of publication:	*1990.*
Call number date:	*2000.*

Statement on map:	*As at 1-1-85.*
Date of publication:	*1986.*
Call number date:	*1985.*

Title:	*Arlington County eighteenth century.*
Date of publication:	*1990.*
Call number date:	*17--.*

(See other examples for specific situations on page 1.17 in the *Map Cataloging Manual.*) The Library of Congress defines "date of situation" as "the date in the call number [that] represents the date of information or situation, not the date of publication" and goes on to state explicitly that "[i]f there is no indication of the date of situation on the item, it is usually assumed to be the same as the publication date."

It pays to look at every piece of information on a map, no matter how small the type, in terms of finding at least an inferred date of situation (and/or publication), or even figuring out a particular year based on some deductive reasoning. It turns out that, for city maps in particular, advertisements can be very valuable in this regard. The illustrations used in advertisements of automobiles and clothing styles or even architectural styles can often serve to place the age of a map in a specific context, at least at the decade level. In addition, an advertisement for a business or store sometimes will reveal an inferred year of publication, if not actual date of situation, by providing a year of establishment and then including a banner or headline, such as "In business for 75 years" or "Celebrating 20 years of professional service."

Another extremely important type of information that often will provide a logical date of situation or publication is printer/publisher codes. For instance, Rand McNally, General Drafting Company, and

H. M. Gousha all use(d) a numeric or alphanumeric code that provides the date of publication by year, and even in some cases by month. Rand McNally's and H. M. Gousha's were truly codes, meaning that you needed to understand the significance of the numbers, and sometimes also letters, in each code in order to tell which year the map was produced. For many years these were considered "company secrets," but translation tables and explanations for these and other companies' codes are available both in hard-copy form, as articles contributed to the Western Association of Map Libraries' (WAML) *Information Bulletin* and the Special Libraries Association (SLA) Geography and Map Division's (SLA G&M) *Bulletin,* and, more conveniently, in electronic form at <http://www.waml.org/datecode.html>. Other well-known codes that provide year or month-and-year information include those found on Central Intelligence Agency (CIA) maps from the 1970s to the present, and on items derived from the Government Printing Office (GPO) for federal agency maps. The CIA codes changed in form from the 1970s to the 1980s by becoming more detailed, but the GPO codes have retained a similar structure and appearance over many decades and always start with something such as "[star]GPO:" or "U.S. Government Printing Office: . . ."

These and other situations and quirks are covered in detail in the LC *Map Cataloging Manual,* and, therefore, I will not go into further details. Suffice it to say that, at the very least, in all but rare occasions, an inferred date of situation can be determined for a map.

One other point must be made in relation to the date of situation, and that has to do with providing justification in the bibliographic record when the date of situation differs from the publication date. Again, from the *Map Cataloging Manual* comes this advice: "When the date in the call number differs from the publication date, the cataloging record must contain some justification for the discrepancy, whether in the title, edition statement, statement of responsibility, notes, etc." (p. 1.17).

Scale Statement in the Call Number for Map Series or Collections

Whenever you are cataloging a map series or collection, the date of situation does not apply because specific sheets in the group may represent cartographic information from differing times. The only possible way to represent such a situation is to give a range of years, and that simply is not part of the system developed for map call numbers.

Instead, and in place of the year in the call number, an abbreviated form of the scale for the series or collection is given. This designation is composed of the lowercase letter "s" followed by the denominator of the representative fraction in the scale minus the last three digits, and a comma is never used in the designation. (An earlier practice, which you may have noticed was used on some maps in your collection, was to place the "s" immediately following the classification number and then the scale abbreviation on the next line.) If the series or collection is at a scale larger than 1:1,000 the denominator is treated as a decimal unit and is preceded by one or more zeros. The following example, with the exception of the bracketed scales that I have provided for clarity, comes from the LC *Map Cataloging Manual* (p. 1.18) and it clearly shows the treatment described:

Scale	Scale Symbol
1:80	s008
1:800	s08
1:7,850	s7
1:50,750	s50
[1:150,000	s150]
[1:1,000,000	s1000]
1:150,000,000	s150000

If the scale is one in which a representative fraction is not provided, such as "Scale not given" or "Not drawn to scale," then three zeros are used after the letter "s", e.g., s000.

If the map series or collection is composed of maps drawn at two scales, determine the predominant scale used in the set and give that scale as shown in the previous example. If the maps are at three or more scales, i.e., the scale statement reads "Scales differ," then use the designation "svar."

Author Cutter

The last element in the call number is the author cutter, unless the map is a reproduction, in which case the year of the reproduced map is given. The author cutter is usually a two-place alphanumeric designation, such as .U5 for names beginning with "United States" or .S6 for the personal name of "Smith, John P." To prevent duplicate call numbers from being established, additional numbers can be added to extend the author cutter. Naturally, the author cutter is based on the authorized form of the name found in the Main Entry or on the first significant word in the title should the record be created using title main entry.

To create an author cutter, see the "Item Cutter" table (p. 1.19) in the LC *Map Cataloging Manual* or the "LC Basic Cutter Table" in the *Library of Congress Cataloging Service Bulletin* (No. 104, May 1972), which are the same but given in different order. To see the same tables that also include a methodology for expanding author cutters to accommodate similar forms of names, use the Library of Congress's *Subject Cataloging Manual: Shelflisting,* Section G 60 (p. 14) or the one found in *A Guide to the Library of Congress Classification* (Chan, 1999, p. 69).

Second Date for Reproductions

As outlined at the beginning of this chapter, a reproduction, facsimile, or reprint of a map receives two dates in the call number, the first for the date of situation of the original and the second for the date of reproduction. This is spelled out clearly in the "Classification" chapter in the LC *Map Cataloging Manual:* "Facsimiles and formally published reprints receive a second date as the final element of the call number. This date, which follows the item Cutter, is the date of publication of the facsimile or reprint.

> EXAMPLE:
> G4314.C5A3 1882 .S7 1967
> A facsimile of an 1882 bird's-eye view of Colorado Springs published in 1967." (p. 1.21)

Note that the LC statement says "formally published"; this is meant to separate Xerox and other forms of mechanical copies of maps, such as blue-line prints, from this category of publication. Mechanically reproduced maps, such as blue-line and black-line prints and Xerox copies, are treated as originals or surrogates for originals and thus are cataloged using only the date of situation. As denoted in the section on "Photocopies" in the LC *Map Cataloging Manual:*

AACR2 defines photocopy as "a macroform photoreproduction produced directly on opaque materials by radiant energy through contact or projection." . . . Under this policy, photocopies are considered separate items in their own right and are described following the general rules for cartographic materials. (p. 8.7)

Serial Map Designation in the Call Number

Although this book does not cover map serials, a brief indication of what happens to designate a map serial title in the call number seems warranted. Quite simply, for a map serial title, the date of situation is replaced by the word "year" in the call number. All of the other call number components remain the same. Naturally, the specific items would each be marked with their year of publication so that they can be filed in chronological order in the drawers.

CREATING A LIBRARY OF CONGRESS CALL NUMBER

Although the classification G-Schedule is but one component of the entire LC classification system, it is unique in that one must learn its inherent meaning through a specific methodology. The components of the call number, which includes up to two types of "cutters," or more accurately one cutter and one code, when combined allow the call number to represent a specific geographic area and type of map. Learning the methodology and construct of the G call number is necessary in order to apply it correctly. Key to understanding geographic area and/or type of map is the value of the fourth digit in the classification number.

Since the fourth digit in the classification number in the G-class determines the meaning involved for the entire call number (i.e., as to whether it represents a general versus topical map and also the geographical level, such as a country, nonpolitical geographic region or area, a political area, such as a county, or a city), an illustration to assist in learning the basics of call number creation is given here. The hierarchy of classification numbers represents the most general to the most complex situations using a single state in the United States and subdividing the state accordingly into its smaller geographic components. Interspersed in its proper sequence, following a call number for a general map, are call numbers for topical maps of a specific geographic location, for example, a geologic map of Pennsylvania, a tourist map of a county in Pennsylvania, and a map showing the bus routes and lines within a Pennsylvania city.

G3820	General map of Pennsylvania
G3821.C5	Map of Pennsylvania showing a specific topic such as geology
G3822.P6	General map of the Pocono Mountains in Pennsylvania
G3822.P6E63	Recreational map of the Pocono Mountains in Pennsylvania
G3823.C4	General map of Centre County, Pennsylvania
G3823.C4E635	Tourist map of Centre County, Pennsylvania
G3824.P5	General map of Philadelphia, Pennsylvania
G3824.P5P22	Transit (bus system) map of Philadelphia, Pennsylvania

Note the use of geographic and/or subject cutters in the second through eighth classification numbers, such as the C5 subject cutter for geology and the P6 geographic cutter for the Pocono Mountains. Once again, the geographic area cutter always comes before a subject cutter in those cases where both are needed.

Not shown in the previous illustration are the date of situation, or scale designation if needed, the author cutter, and whether the map is a facsimile or other reproduction, a second date representing the reproduced version of the map, to complete an entire call number.

CONCLUSION

With practice and patience you will find that the creation of a G-class call number becomes pretty straightforward and the meaning of each of its components becomes clear. That is not to say that the system does not have its own weaknesses and/or shortcomings. One of these shortcomings is that the list of subject cutters needs to be expanded or clarified. Susan Moore (1999) discusses this topic in the section "Problems in Using the G-Schedule." In fact, Moore makes it clear that Chapter 1, "Classification" in the LC *Map Cataloging Manual* is an absolute must-have reference source for learning how to create

G-class call numbers because it explains in detail many of the idiosyncrasies involved.

As just mentioned, the excellent article by Susan Moore is well worth reading as a companion to this chapter's brief overview. It can be found in either *Cataloging and Classification Quarterly,* 27(3/4), pp. 385-404, or in the quarterly's companion monograph publication, *Maps and Related Cartographic Materials: Cataloging, Classification, and Bibliographic Control* (Andrew and Larsgaard, 1999), on the same pages. Her article describes how the G-Schedule methodically divides up the world into smaller pieces, explains how the schedule works, reproduces the subject cutter table list of alphanumeric designations found in the G-Schedule, and provides more background on this topic. The bibliography to this article is a "Who's Who" resource of LC classification practice, in general, and classification practices for map collections, specifically.

Chapter 16

A Quick Look at Subject Analysis for Maps

One of the last components of the bibliographic record is the subject area. This area is very important in terms of the way most patrons approach and use a given online public access catalog (OPAC) in their attempts to find a map. Several articles and books relating to reference service for map collections have consistently shown that map library patrons attempt to find maps for their needs based on requests that begin, "I need a map of [a given geographic area]." Therefore, subject analysis for maps naturally focuses first on geographic area but also may need to include topics, since many maps do explicitly have a primary topic associated with them, such as topography or geology.

Subject analysis itself is not the most difficult part of the cataloger's job in this area of the record; after all, the map's title and content often prove feasible enough at least to provide a straightforward geographic subject heading. In fact, providing a geographic subject heading for a general map of a continent, country, province, state, county, or city is very straightforward and takes the form of the following:

> Pennsylvania – Maps.
> France – Maps.
> Europe – Maps.

More difficult for the cataloger new to subject access for sheet maps is providing the correct form of geographic headings and employing their correct usage as a geographic subdivision.

Once we cross the line from a general map to a topic-based map, e.g., a road map of the United States, or from a single map to multiple maps, the challenge quickly begins! We approach subject analysis for maps on two fronts: by talking about what to consider during the subject analysis process, including looking at publisher's intent in determining the primary topic involved, and by looking at those aspects related to the assignment, i.e., their layout, of the geographic headings and subdivisions themselves.

Keep in mind that we are using the *Library of Congress Subject Headings* thesaurus, herein referred to as LCSH, and will focus on the use of subject headings from this source. If you do not have access to this title in hard-copy form or as a part of *Cataloger's Desktop,* fear not. Another way to access specific subject headings is by using the Library of Congress Name Authority File (LCNAF or LCAF), found on OCLC.

Finally, it is extremely important to stay on top of geographic names when working with maps and atlases because new place names are created and old place names change due to the outcome of political conquests or new discoveries. The source of names for places in the United States and its territories and Antarctica is the U.S. Board on Geographic Names' (BGN) Geographic Names Information System (GNIS) database. The source of names for places outside the United States is the National Imagery and Mapping Agency's (NIMA) GEOnet Names Server (GNS) database. Additional authoritative sources for geographic names are the *Merriam-Webster's Geographical Dictionary* and the *Rand McNally Commercial Atlas and Marketing Guide,* among others. All of these sources are given in Chapter 3, "Necessary Tools of the Trade." Keeping abreast of geographic subject heading changes can also be done by regularly perusing the *L.C. Subject Headings Weekly Lists* as well as the Library of Congress's *Cataloging Service Bulletin.*

In addition, it is absolutely necessary to have access to a copy of the Library of Congress's *Subject Cataloging Manual: Subject Headings* (SCM), as this is the tool that breaks down and explains the methodology inherent in the construct of geographic subject heading, and also geographic subdivision, policies and practice. The SCM also provides lists of "free-floating subdivisions" under section H 1095, which is the most heavily used and applicable list of subdivisions for maps, as well as other such lists that will be discussed in the following.

Additional reference sources that assist in subject heading and/ or subdivision application include the Library of Congress's *Free-Floating Subdivisions: An Alphabetical Index* and *LC Period Sub-*

divisions Under Names of Places; Lois Mai Chan's *Library of Congress Subject Headings: Principles and Applications;* and, perhaps most important, the Library of Congress, Geography and Map Division's *Map Cataloging Manual,* which I will refer to as the MCM.

SUBJECT ANALYSIS FOR SHEET MAPS

Subject analysis for sheet maps parallels the practice used for other materials; i.e., the cataloger must peruse the content of the item in order to provide one or more subject headings that reflect what that item is about. The difference in the subject analysis process between a sheet map and a book is that it may take a bit longer to do this exercise with a map. One must not only consider a close inspection of the cartographic content itself but review and take into account one or more titles and give consideration to additional information found with the map, such as text, tables, indexes, inset and/or ancillary maps, and potentially even such mundane items as advertisements. For a book, the process entails reviewing the table of contents and title, along with a quick review of the overall content, to provide one or more subject headings. Another inherent difference is that subject analysis for a map must be done for geographic area *and* potentially one or more topics, while analysis of a book focuses on topics, only some of which may contain a geographic area.

One of the most frequently heard questions about subject headings has to do with the "correct" number to give in the bibliographic record, often phrased as, "Is there a maximum number of headings that should be given?" Generally, a self-imposed maximum number of subject headings for maps does not exist; what is important is to give the geographic area covered by the map as a subject heading, at a minimum. Perhaps the best source to turn to for answering the previous question is the MCM, where in Chapter 4, "Subject Analysis," it states, "There is no limit imposed on the number of subject headings that can be given to a particular item for full-level cataloging, provided they are properly applied." The "properly applied" portion of the statement is the crux of subject analysis for maps.

A very useful way to approach analyzing the content of a map is outlined in the MCM. It states that "[t]he first step in subject analysis of an item is to eliminate peripheral material from consideration"

(p. 4.2). This is simply applying common sense, for if we eliminate from consideration such things as small areas surrounding the primary place that has been mapped, then this allows us to focus on providing the correct subject heading(s) for the area in question. The example given is of maps of West Virginia that also typically display portions of Virginia and Maryland; the portions of the adjacent states can be excluded from subject analysis. If the map is a general map of West Virginia, then the subject heading of "West Virginia – Maps" can be provided, or even if it *is* about a specific topic related to West Virginia, one still focuses on giving only the topical subject heading subdivided by West Virginia.

Another way to approach this is to examine the cartographic information separately from all other information and then consider what noncartographic items should not have a bearing on the subject analysis. For example, National Geographic maps typically have a number of small historical notes associated with particular places on the maps. These may not be substantial enough to have any bearing on the subject analysis of the maps themselves.

In fact, the first three pages of Chapter 4 in the MCM are an excellent guide toward learning the parameters of subject analysis for maps. The specific units involved include the proper order of subject headings and the subject analysis process itself, each with clear examples to follow. Once again, common sense prevails: "The first subject heading should always be the one that most nearly corresponds to the classification number (i.e., the heading that represents the predominant topic of the work)," but consideration is given to the not so obvious as well. Concerns such as how to provide subject headings for more than one geographic area and, more important, for three or more geographic areas, are reviewed. A quick overview of the primary points given in this unit of MCM reveals these guides:

- Subject analysis influences both the classification and the subject headings provided for the item and may indirectly influence the provision of some notes in the record.
- While classification serves the purpose of keeping maps of a geographic area together, including those maps of a general nature as well as those with specific topics, subject headings serve the same purpose, except that they keep subject entries that provide access to the maps together in the catalog.

- Subject analysis of a map should be as specific as the item warrants, which is to say, try not to overanalyze the intent of the map.
- Subject analysis is based on what an item is, not on what it says that it is. Rely on the cartographic content first and foremost but always consider publisher's intent as well (more on that later).
- "Every map of an identifiable place must have a subject heading for the area. Maps of places that cannot be identified receive no geographic subject headings." The former part of this statement is rather obvious, although consider that a topical subject heading with a geographic subdivision also fulfills this requirement in our electronic age. The latter part of the statement is one in which I have no experience but does give pause for thought, as this does occur.
- A map of three places is classified for the overall geographic area that contains the three places but does not need to have a broader subject heading if the subject headings for the three places are individually provided. (A map of two places naturally would receive two geographic subject headings, or subdivisions if applied to a topical heading, one for each place.)
- A general map may also receive a secondary subject tracing, if warranted, as long as the second (topical) subject is not subsumed by the concept of the more general (usually geographic) heading.
- A map of a broad subject receives the subject heading that corresponds to that overall subject; more specific subjects are not necessary, except if they can be justified based on wording in the title, if the more specific information was overprinted on the map that primarily is about the broader subject, or if other separate information is part of the map, such as a separate legend, ancillary map, inset, or text about the specific subject only. The MCM uses the example of a tectonic map of France in which earthquake information is also supplied as a circumstance where you would add the more specific subject heading for the earthquake.
- All subject headings given for a map must be justified elsewhere in the record, such as information that appears in the title, as part of a series heading, or in the call number or notes.

Finally, a "Subject Heading Decision Table" and a very helpful list of "Special Applications and Instructions" concludes the rest of Chapter 4. The special applications area reviews specific subject headings and how they should be applied and also discusses the differences between ancillary, inset, and subsidiary maps compared to main maps and how they should be handled in terms of subject analysis. You should become intimately familiar with this chapter and the related chapter on classification (Chapter 1) in the MCM, as they both provide a welcoming place to learn about subject analysis for maps.

Publisher's Intent

We first touched upon publisher's intent in Chapter 15 while discussing subject codes in the G-class call number. After all, one of the tenets of bringing together like maps in the map collection is to provide a subject code in the call number that corresponds to the primary subject heading used in the record.

To review quickly, publisher's intent is most readily determined by the title of the map and the specific words in the title and/or their layout. Compare the title information with what is shown cartographically to judge the accuracy of the title as to intent. Other nongeographic components of the item may also be helpful in determining, or ruling out, what the map is about. Such items as indexes to tourist or historical locations in a city or region may make a difference in determining whether a map is a general one of a city/region or, when combined with title information, truly is meant to be used by visitors, i.e., tourists, as a "tourist map."

GEOGRAPHIC SUBJECT HEADINGS

Although a cataloger new to working with maps might easily learn the structure of geographic subject headings solely by observing their format when used for general maps of a single place, attempting to learn the idiosyncrasies of these types of subject headings for more complex maps is nearly impossible. One must have the Library of Congress's *Subject Cataloging Manual: Subject Headings,* or SCM, in order to learn the correct assignment of a geographic subject heading and its related subheadings. We will follow the guidelines in the

SCM to learn the critically important concepts of "first-order political divisions," qualifying geographic headings, and indirect/direct subdivision of topical subject headings with geographic headings. The same reference source is used to explain form subdivisions used under geographic headings for maps.

As a bit of background, the opening paragraph in SCM's H 690 describes formulating geographic subject headings very nicely: "Headings for geographic names fall into two categories: (1) names of political jurisdictions and (2) non-jurisdictional geographic names." This allows us to look at the "world" of geographic subject headings in a particular way and introduces the notion that because LC has placed all geographic places in these two categories, they will be treated differently in particular circumstances. This means that particular jurisdictions, such as cities, counties, and countries, are "names," whereas islands, mountains, oceans, and other geographic features are "subjects" and are tagged in the catalog record according, as shown in H 405.

Instruction sheet H 690 also describes when to use the English form of a place name versus the vernacular form, when to use abbreviations as opposed to spelled-out words in a name such as "Saint" and "St.," and how to handle initial articles in a name; it also provides examples showing cross-references from various forms of the geographic heading chosen.

Qualification of Geographic Subject Headings

The extremely important concept of qualifying place names is discussed fully in instruction sheet H 810 in the SCM. To specify a particular place in a geographic subject heading, that place needs to be "qualified" by the use of a political jurisdiction. This is most important when more than one place has the same name, but the practice of qualifying geographic headings transcends this specific need. Using a qualifier allows each geographic heading to be unique to the place that it represents on the map or with any other form of material. The place name in parentheses, i.e., the qualifier, allows you to distinguish between places such as Alexandria (Va.) and Alexandria (Egypt), or Paris (Tex.) and Paris (France).

The *General rule* in this instruction sheet is to "[q]ualify subject headings representing geographic entities by the name of the country or countries in which they are located, except for the following . . .". The exceptions are six countries for which we *do not qualify* a place by the name of the country. Instead, in those six instances, which will be outlined momentarily, a place is qualified by that country's "first-order political division."

The six countries that are exceptions to using the country as the qualifier and their first order political divisions used as the qualifier in these cases are:

Country	Level of Qualification
Australia	state
Canada	province
Great Britain	constituent country
Malaysia	state
United States	state
Yugoslavia	republic

That is to say, if you are using a geographic heading for a place in any of these six countries, then that place will be qualified by the name of a state, province, constituent country, or republic as opposed to the name of the country as a whole. For instance, the name of a city or county in the United States is qualified by the name of the state in which it resides, such as: Pittsburgh (Pa.) and Clarke County (Ga.). The name of a city in Canada is qualified by the province in which it resides, e.g., Montreal (Quebec), and so forth. This practice also applies to nonpolitical places; for instance, the correct form of the heading for Lake Chelan in Washington State is Chelan, Lake (Wash.). Note that the name of the country or first-order political division used as a qualifier is placed within parentheses following the place name and, in many cases, may be abbreviated.

The remainder of H 810 goes into great detail as to how to qualify names for places in two and more than two jurisdictions, abbreviation practices for qualifier names, qualifying places at various levels of jurisdiction, etc. In addition, the actual form of the qualifier as to its spelled-out versus abbreviated form is provided in a list for each of the six exceptional countries. Once you learn the six exceptional countries and the jurisdictional levels used as the qualifiers of place in each of those countries, you will find that providing the correct form of a geographic heading is greatly simplified.

First-Order Political Divisions of Countries

The concept of "first-order political divisions of countries" has to do with the names of these units, such as states, provinces, divisions, or departments, and how they are used in formulating a heading. Instruction sheet H 713 in SCM identifies these. Basically, when subdividing a topical subject heading by a geographic heading or name, one uses the first-order political division of the country involved in the form of [topic] – [place]. For instance, for a work about boating in Michigan, the topical heading of "Boats and boating" would be subdivided by the first-order political division in the United States, which is a state, in this case Michigan. It would appear in the record as follows:

Boats and boating – Michigan.

Naturally, if the work is about boating in the United States, then you would provide the geographic subdivision of "United States" in this case. The concept of first-order political divisions is important and will become more apparent with practice in assigning geographic headings and subdivisions.

GEOGRAPHIC SUBDIVISIONS FOR TOPICAL SUBJECT HEADINGS

Indirect Subdivision Practice

It is probably safe to say that the majority of topical subject headings in LCSH can be subdivided geographically, i.e., by the name of a place. This practice allows a particular subject to be tied to one or more places where it occurs. Instruction sheet H 830 covers the practice of "Indirect Local Subdivision," which is to say, by applying the name of a country or first-order political division following the subject heading in question, but before the local place, such as a city, or nonpolitical entity, such as a river valley or island:

> The term (May Subd Geog) is an instruction appearing after many subject headings in the SUBJECTS file allowing those headings to be subdivided geographically by interposing the name of a country (or in certain instances the first order political division) between the subject heading and the name of the place within that country or state to which the subject is limited.

"May Subd Geog" is coded in the subject authority record as "i" in the 008/06 field and is shown in the OCLC system's fixed field as "Geo Subd".

The *General provision* given in H 830 states:

> When a heading is coded (May Subd Geog) [in LCSH], subdivide locally by interposing the name of the relevant country between the heading and the name of any territorial entity falling wholly within the country, including: subordinate political jurisdictions, such as provinces, districts, counties, cities, etc.; historic kingdoms, principalities, etc.; geographic features and regions, such as mountain ranges, bodies of water, lake regions, watersheds, metropolitan areas, etc.; [and] islands situated within the territorial limits of the country in question.

For example:

> Roads – Italy – Rome Metropolitan Area – Maps.
> Geology – Ethiopia – Addis Ababa Region – Maps.
> Phytogeography – France – Gironde – Maps.

Specific applications are also given in this instruction sheet for situations such as how to divide historic kingdoms and other like entities that lie wholly within a modern jurisdiction, use of the latest name of a place and present territorial sovereignties, and metropolitan city areas and regions.

An extremely important part of this instruction goes back, once again, to those six exceptional countries listed previously and using their first-order political divisions as the interposing heading. These are denoted under a category labeled "Exceptions," which is very detailed and shows how to subdivide further these first-order political divisions, if needed, by using the name of a city, county, or other subordinate unit; when and how to use recognized political regions of a country, such as southern or northern California; etc. Perhaps the two most important things to learn, next to formatting the subdivisions, are that one may *subdivide a topic using only up to two levels of jurisdiction*—"Construct headings with no more than two levels of geographic subdivision, using the country (or the first order political division in the case of the four exceptions discussed in sec. 5.a., below) as the collecting level"—and the lowest level that can be used to subdivide is the city—"Divide topics geographically to a level no lower than that of a city, town, etc." (Those "four exceptions discussed in sec. 5.a." are actually three and are listed as (1) Canada, divide through the name of a province; (2) Great Britain, divide through the name of a constituent country; and (3) the United States, divide through the name of a state.)

Study H 830 thoroughly, but keep in mind that recalling the six exceptional countries also carries one quite far in learning how to assign indirect subdivisions correctly.

Direct Subdivision Practice

In certain cases topical subject headings are subdivided by using what is called "direct geographic subdivision" practice to specify the location of the topic involved without having to interpose the first-order political division between the topic and the place. Beginning in November 1976, this practice was terminated with some small exceptions. This now very uncommon practice occurs with only two specific cities and a city that is considered a country, as outlined in H 830.d:

> Cities assigned directly after topics. Assign the names of the following cities directly after topics: Jerusalem (see H 980); Washington, D.C. (see H 1050). . . . Note: Since Vatican City (see H 1045) is treated as a country rather than a city, it is also assigned directly after topics without interposing the name of the larger geographic entity

This practice applies to certain types of geographic entities, as noted in the following. Until February 1996, New York City was also used directly after a topical subject heading but now is treated as other cities in New York State, see H 990 for instructions on using New York City.

An example of a place name without a geographic qualifier that would be used directly to subdivide a topical heading might be "Mississippi River," which is not qualified because it flows through several political jurisdictions, in this case states in the United States. Names of certain islands also are used directly, instead of indirectly through the name of a country.

Other exceptions to indirect subdivision practice, outlined in H 830 include 5.b, Inverted headings for regions and 5.c, Regions larger than countries. Section 5.c stipulates, "Use the name of any jurisdiction or region that does not lie wholly within a single existing country (or first order political division of the three exceptional countries . . .) directly after topics." This includes "the names of the three exceptional countries . . ." which are Canada, Great Britain, and the United States; "historic kingdoms, empires, etc., for example, Holy Roman Empire"; and "geographic features and regions such as continents and other major regions, bodies of water, mountain ranges, coasts, etc., for example, Europe, Great Lakes . . .". The key phrase in Section 5.c is "that does not lie wholly within a single existing country (or first order political division of the three exceptional countries . . .)," hence the Mississippi River example provided earlier.

Free-Floating Subdivisions for Geographic Headings

A list of free-floating subdivisions specific to geographic headings is given in instruction sheet H 1140. The most common of these are the form headings that describe what type of material the geographic heading is being applied to: "Maps," "Maps, Physical," "Maps, Topographic," and the other similar forms. See this instruction sheet for the entire list and pay attention to those terms which are footnoted because the footnotes tell you specifically how the headings can be used.

Bodies of water have specific instructions for use as free-floating headings. Turn to H 1145.5 when applying certain free-floating headings that can be used with places such as rivers, lakes, watersheds, and oceans.

CONCLUSION

Although the previous discussion only highlights the more important aspects of subject analysis and geographic subject headings as they relate to maps, hopefully, it imparts a foundation from which to build a body of knowledge. As with all other portions of map cataloging, working with the maps themselves to gain experience in applying these and other practices is the best way to become adept at creating accurate and complete bibliographic records for maps.

Allow me to point you to an excellent and very helpful article on this topic titled "Subject Analysis for Cartographic Materials," by Katherine H. Weimer (1999), which can be found in either *Cataloging and Classification Quarterly,* 27(3/4), pp. 385-404, or in the quarterly's companion monograph publication, *Maps and Related Cartographic Materials: Cataloging, Classification, and Bibliographic Control* (Andrew and Larsgaard, 1999), on the same pages. She not only takes care of describing the two sides of subject analysis for maps, geographic area and topics, but also covers the correct order of subject headings, writes about the role of authorized headings, and provides a table at the end that matches form subdivision headings to subject cutters found in the LC G-Schedule. I strongly encourage reading this article to enhance your understanding of subject analysis for maps.

Chapter 17

Added Entries in the Record

As alluded to in Chapter 8, many times, the creation of a particular map is the result of multiple individuals or corporate bodies, or a combination of both, each being responsible for one or more of the tasks involved in the final work. Therefore, once we determine who was primarily responsible for the map, or if no person or body is named on the map as being responsible for its creation, the next decision is whether to provide added entries for either the other individuals or bodies responsible and/or for additional titles. The following circumstances, according to AACR2R, warrant added entries in the record:

- a person or corporate body has been chosen as the main entry and there are other persons and/or bodies named prominently on the map; and
- the number of persons or bodies are too numerous or diffuse to make a main entry determination; therefore, title is used as the main entry, but one or more persons or bodies are named prominently.

Also, added entries can be given when there are other titles to choose from or the chosen title proper can be delivered in a different manner due to typography or layout, using the 246 field. In each of these situations, we need to ask whether it is necessary to provide access to any or all of these additional persons, bodies, or titles for the benefit of our patrons and other catalogers.

Following Rule 21.29C in AACR2R, once the main entry has been determined, trace for all other meaningful personal or corporate bodies or additional titles, "if some catalogue users might suppose that the description of an item would be found under that heading or title rather than under the heading or title chosen for the main entry." In the context of sheet maps, any person, company, or agency that is known to have ties to the creation, production, or publication of maps would qualify for added entry status under this rule. Rule 21.29B instructs to make these added entries for persons or bodies as delineated in the "Specific Rules" listed under 21.30, which includes pertinent instructions for maps under Rule 21.30A, "Two or more persons or bodies involved"; Rule 21.30D, "Editors and compilers"; Rule 21.30E, "Corporate bodies"; and the last paragraph, Rule 21.30J. The following discussions are based on these rules for persons, corporate bodies, titles, and additional situations.

OTHER PERSONAL NAMES

Although the majority of maps do not name individuals responsible for some or all of the cartographic work involved in producing a map, in those cases where individuals are named, they should be traced. Chapter 8, "Main Entry and Statement of Responsibility" discussed giving main entry status to a person formally named in the statement of responsibility as being responsible for the creation of the map.

According to Rule 21.30A, if one, two, or three other persons are identified as having a role in the map's creation, they also should be traced as added entries using the 700 field. If four or more other persons are identified, then trace for only the first-named person in this group. Roles that identify work accomplished on a given map beyond that of cartographer include that of surveyors, field checkers, compilers, and editors, among others. Follow Rule 21.30D for editors and compilers in those two specific instances, and for other situations follow Rule 21.30A.

OTHER CORPORATE BODIES

Follow Rule 21.30E1 about added entries for corporate bodies:

Make an added entry under the heading for a prominently named corporate body, unless it functions solely as distributor or manufacturer. Make an added entry under a prominently named publisher if the responsibility for the work extends beyond that of merely publishing it. In case of doubt, make an added entry.

For more information about tracing for cartographic publishers, see the separate section later in the chapter. Thankfully, the last sentence in this rule allows the added entry to be made even when the cataloger lacks enough explicit information to make an absolute determination that the publisher is responsible for more than just the publishing aspect, because this is often the case with maps.

Also, as in the case stated for persons previously, if one, two, or three other corporate bodies are involved in the creation of the map, provide added entries for each, but if four or more bodies, then provide an added entry for the first named in the group, if that can be determined from the arrangement or layout of the corporate bodies listed.

OTHER TITLES

Under the rule for added entries for titles, Rule 21.30J, the last paragraph states, "If considered necessary for access, make an added entry for any version of the title (cover title, caption title, running title) that, according to 21.2A, does not constitute a change in the title proper." Little discussion will be provided here because the circumstances for providing other added titles for maps are elucidated in Chapter 9, "Providing a Title for the Record." Significant differences to the title proper, as given in Rule 21.2A, include whether any important words in the title proper are added, deleted, or changed, and a change in the order of the first five words, not including initial articles, prepositions, or conjunctions.

The particular circumstance not touched upon for maps in either of the previous rules has to do with the layout or typography of a single title, which may signal a different way of reading the title and also should be considered as a title added entry.

TRACING FOR CARTOGRAPHIC PUBLISHERS

Tracing for a cartographic publisher as an added entry differs from that for monograph publishers because publishers of monographs typically fulfill only the publishing role. The circumstance given in Rule 21.30E for corporate bodies—"Make an added entry under a prominently named publisher"—often applies to cartographic publishers, as well as to those of other formats of materials, such as audiovisual, and thus map publishers may be traced in the record.

After gaining experience in cataloging maps, the common map publishers/producers of the twentieth century become quite recognizable, even as the number of these continues to dwindle due to mergers with and/or buyouts by the larger publishers, such as Rand McNally or MapQuest.com. Names of companies such as General Drafting Company, Hagstrom Maps, H. M. Gousha Company, Arrow Map Company, Champion Map Corporation, the American Automobile Association, and King of the Road Maps, among many others, will become commonplace the more maps that one catalogs and the older the maps themselves are. Many of these companies no longer exist, but the key point is that when the map was created they *did* exist, and if they played a role beyond simply publishing the map, then they should be traced, as these familiar names can be key access points in the search for a particular map.

OTHER POTENTIAL ADDED ENTRIES

It is often helpful to trace for an agency or company responsible for the base map that was used to create the item being cataloged, and this should be done because part of the geographic information on the map was originally created by that other agency or company. Most often in the United States, this turns out to be the U.S. Geological Survey, and a quoted note, such as "Base map by U.S. Geological Survey," provides the justification needed for the added entry. Similar notes regarding a different agency or company are sufficient to consider tracing for the body concerned.

JUSTIFICATION FOR AN ADDED ENTRY

After determining what and who needs to be traced as added entries in the record, the last step is to provide justification for the entries when it is not apparent from the description in the record as to why the individuals or bodies are being traced. Rule 21.29F in AACR2R advises:

> If the reason for an added entry is not apparent from the description (e.g., if a person or body whose name is used as the basis for an added entry heading is not named in a statement of responsibility or in the publication details), provide a note giving, as appropriate, the name of the person or body (see 1.7B6) and/or the title (see 1.7B4).

Often the notes provided are quoted notes so that the bibliographic record user understands that the information provided appears specifically in that form on the map and in fact comes directly from the map. Notes such as "Copyright . . ." and "Base map from . . ." are common in this situation.

SECTION V:
HISTORICAL SHEET MAPS
AND SPECIAL CASES

Chapter 18

Historical Maps—
Specific Points to Consider

Although graphically the same as contemporary maps, other than the change of conventions for things such as symbols and showing relief, historical maps must be described differently in some specific areas of the bibliographic record due to the means by which the maps were produced and who is responsible for producing them. An excellently detailed and very informative article that will assist one in working with historical maps is "Cataloging Early Printed Maps" by Nancy Kandoian (1999), which I highly recommend be read and used while learning to deal with early maps. The following discussion includes some comments to assist those cataloging historical maps, but consider the aforementioned article to be the primary source of information, beyond the standard tools for cataloging maps, regarding the creation of bibliographic records for this genre of maps.

Generally speaking, a "historical," "rare," or "early" map may be defined as one that was produced before 1850. During the nineteenth century, production methods changed from primarily copperplate engraving to manufacturing, more easily and with less expense, by lithography. In addition, a transition took place over time from maps being produced by specific individuals, from manuscript to final output, to being produced by either government/military agencies or commercial companies. This means that the cataloger has to be more aware of the main entry, statement of responsibility, and publication areas and the kind of information that is provided in these areas of the record.

MAIN ENTRY

As mentioned earlier, historical maps were made by and identified as being made by one or more individuals much more commonly than by a particular company or agency. Naturally, the change of attribution from person to company or agency occurred as a progression, along with the change from producing small numbers of maps by copperplate and handpress to mass-producing copies of a map, first, using lithography and then, later, the automated printing press. Thus, Rule 21.1A in AACR2R for using the name of a person for main entry purposes comes into effect while cataloging a historical map. Many of the more prominent cartographers of historical maps are well-documented individuals such as Gerardus Mercator, Abraham Ortelius, John Speed, and others. Provide the heading for the individual as the main entry when that individual is identified in the title and/or statement of responsibility on the map.

DETERMINING THE TITLE PROPER

A common occurrence with historical maps is long, sometimes complex titles. Perhaps a more accurate statement is that one must frequently determine what constitutes the title proper versus other title information. Second, another common feature on early maps is the appearance of what might be considered a second title, usually within its own cartouche or border and separated from the formal title statement, which often turns out to be a dedication or statement honoring a noted ruler or military leader, or perhaps the person who funded the creation of the map. Using this as a working context, Rules 1B13, 1B14, and 1B15 in *Cartographic Materials* provide some guidance as to determining the title proper for early maps; Rule 1B14 specifically assists us with the latter case noted earlier.

Rule 1B13 applies to a title proper that may be abridged. It provides the option to omit any alternative title and its connecting word "or," whether it is in English or in another language, replacing the omitted text with the mark of omission (. . .). However, this rule also refers us to Rule 1B4, which reminds us never to omit the first five words of the title proper. (This is derived from Rule 1.1B4 in AACR2R.)

Another chunk of title may be omitted according to Rule 1B14. Any mottoes, quotations, dedications, or statements that are physically separate from the title proper may be omitted, with the stipulation that the mark of omission not be used in this case. Instead of the mark of omission, give such mottoes, quotations, dedications, or statements as quoted notes in the record. Once you have worked with a few early maps, you will quickly realize how common such things as dedications and quotations are, either as part of their titles or given separately on the map.

Finally, Rule 1B15 tells us, "Do not treat additions to the title, even if they are linked to it by a preposition, conjunction, prepositional phrase, etc., as part of the title proper." What is difficult here is the lack of a clear definition of "additions to the title," although the example used does help. The accompanying APPLICATION, which states, "If such additions to the title constitute a formal statement of the contents of the work, however, record them in a note," provides a means for including such additions to the title in the record.

STATEMENT(S) OF RESPONSIBILITY

Historical maps more regularly identify the individual(s) responsible for all or part of the production of the map involved, commonly using descriptive terms such as "engraved by" or "drawn and engraved by." An exception to this situation is historical maps removed from atlases. These maps may lack such identifying information as to who was involved in their production. However, since many early maps are also in languages such as Latin, one needs to be aware of Latin variations of English terms indicating responsibility, or their abbreviations, to decipher a statement of responsibility. One such term is "delineated" or "delineated by," which in Latin would be "delineavit" or abbreviated as "del." The following list of descriptive terms, although not comprehensive, will help identify the individuals responsible for the map and who should be listed as the main and added entries for the bibliographic record:

Cartography by (*delineavit* or *del.*)
Drafted by (or *draughtsman*)
Engraved by (*sculpsit* or *sculp.*, etc.)
Drawn by
Sketched by
Printed by (*excudit* or *exc.*, etc.)

See also the Library of Congress Geography and Map Division's *Map Cataloging Manual* (p. 2.2) for other "Latin Terms or Contractions" commonly found on historical maps.

Keep in mind that, historically, the various functions that go into the making of a map rested on the shoulders of one or more individuals. It is important, therefore, to provide access to all, or nearly all, individuals who played a role in the creation of these maps. This means understanding that, for example, the role of the printer is much more prominent in this context than in today's world, and the individuals who did the engraving and printing steps of the process should be given in the statement of responsibility and the publisher statement, respectively, and also traced as added entries.

Finally, another change in this area is that it is acceptable to record titles of honor or distinction, such as *Sir* or *Honorable,* as opposed to the rules for contemporary maps.

MATHEMATICAL DATA

Although the overall process for determining scale, projection, and coordinates remains the same as for contemporary maps, one must be aware of the changes as to how distance was measured historically, e.g., using "rods" or "chains" as opposed to feet and miles, and the difference in prime meridian. Each of these takes time to understand and knowledge of where to find equivalencies for historical information compared to today's is of great help. Let's examine each of these areas separately.

Scale Information

As mentioned earlier, lengths used for measurement of distances have changed over time, along with their names, and, thankfully, they have also become more standardized. In working with historical maps, one will commonly find that bar scales are established using the "rod," "pole," or "British nautical mile." So, what do each of these mean in today's common standards of linear measurement such as inches, feet, or miles? One of the best sources of information is Table 1 in Appendix B.3 of *Cartographic Materials,* which shows equivalencies in yards, feet, and inches for fourteen historically common measurement terms. Naturally, you often may be looking to make an equivalent based on miles, but this is simple enough to do once you take the original measurement, such as *x* number of "cables," determine that one cable equals 8,640 inches, and then compare this to the number of inches in one mile. (Remember the powerful number "63360," which is the number of inches in one mile? Dividing 63,360 by 8,640 gives you an equivalent of 7.3 chains per mile; using this based on the bar scale distance given on the map will provide you with a close approximation of the representative fraction to use in the bibliographic record.)

Other sources of distance conversion tables are given in a footnote to Appendix B.2B in *Cartographic Materials* and include the following:

- Doursther, Horace. *Dictionnaire universel des poids et measures anciens et modernes, contenant des tables de monnaies de tous les pays.* Amsterdam: Meridian Publishing Company, 1965.
- Johnstone, William D. *For Good Measure: A Complete Compendium of International Weights and Measures,* First Edition. New York: Holt, Rinehart and Winston, 1975.

Perhaps the most comprehensive online site for these values is at the following Smits site. But, an easier-to-use site is the one developed by Terry Reese, also given here, where you can plug in the numbers and a calculator function does the work for you.

- Smits, Jan. "Mathematical Data for Bibliographic Descriptions." <http://www.kb.nl/kb/resources/frameset_kb.html?/kb/skd/skd/mathemat.html>

  Click on either "Bar Scale Values," which has a good textual description of the topic, or "Petermann's Bar Scale Value," which has a table showing such things as a mile and its equivalent in degrees of longitude and meters, or "Mile," which has an extensive conversion table showing historical and contemporary distance equivalencies for the mile distance based on numerous non-U.S. countries. Perhaps most useful of all is "Geoff Armitage's Conversion Table of Measurements," which lists such things as the English league and the German mile and gives their equivalent measure in millimeters, from which a conversion to other metric measurements can be made.

- Reese, Terry. "Scale Calculator."
  <http://ucs.orst.edu/~reeset/html/scale.html>
  In terms of historical map conversions, this site would best be used in conjunction with one of the online tables in the Smits site or with the table in *Cartographic Materials* to convert the discovered metric value or even inches to a representative fraction.

Projection

Although it did not become common practice to provide the name of the projection used on a map until the twentieth century, occasionally it will be stated on a historical map. Thus, as with contemporary maps, include the name of the projection in the 255 subfield "b" area if it is found on the map.

Providing Coordinates

The major difference between historical and contemporary maps in terms of coordinates is the variety of designated prime meridians, such as "Ferro," or Hierro, the westernmost island in the Canary Islands, used before Greenwich became the de facto prime meridian in 1884. Various countries commonly used the meridian passing through their capital as the prime meridian, or line of origin, for longitude in constructing maps. Therefore, places such as Paris, London, Amsterdam, and Washington, DC, are often denoted as the zero-degree line of longitude on early maps.

> The meridians are all alike, and any one can be chosen as the meridian of origin from which to start the numbering for longitude. The choice became, as might be expected, a problem of international consequence. Numerous countries, each with characteristic national ambition, wished to have 0° longitude within its borders or as the meridian of its capital. For many years each nation published its own maps and charts with longitude reckoned from its own meridian of origin. This, of course, caused much confusion. (Robinson, Sale, and Morrison, 1978, p. 40)

Unfortunately for the map cataloger, this still causes confusion today. The question becomes, "Do you record the coordinates as found on the map being cataloged or convert the historical coordinates to today's measurements and record the contemporary coordinates?" As Nancy Kandoian (1999) so succinctly stated in her article, "One must remember to express longitude coordinates in the mathematical area of a record using Greenwich as the prime meridian, no matter what serves as prime meridian for longitude on the map itself" (Kandoian, 1999, p. 236). To make the transfer from historic to Greenwich prime meridian see Table 3 in Appendix B.3 in *Cartographic Materials,* which shows how many degrees, minutes, and seconds of difference a particular historical prime meridian is from Greenwich. For example, if the map being described has Washington, DC, as the prime meridian, the table shows a difference of 77°00'34" west of Greenwich. This means that you must subtract this amount from both lines of longitude to determine what to put into the bibliographic record. A similar online table can be found at Jan Smits' "Mathematical Data for Bibliographic Descriptions" site listed previously; click on "Geographical Coordinates" and the table titled "Location of Prime Meridians" is a short scroll down the screen.

Another quirk sometimes found on historical maps is indication of two prime meridians, e.g., Paris and Greenwich, one along the top of the map and the other along the bottom. In such a case, use the Greenwich coordinates in the 255 subfield "c" area, *but also* make sure to provide this information in a general note in the form "Paris and Greenwich prime meridians" or "Prime meridians: Paris and Greenwich" or "Prime meridians given as Paris and Greenwich."

PUBLICATION OR PRODUCTION INFORMATION

Because the publishing function is often described on early maps in terms of the related basic functions of printing and selling, the publisher information may appear to be a bit different from that on maps produced in more contemporary times. Therefore, information regarding printers and sellers and their addresses or signs is important to provide, especially if a publisher is not identified. Also, we may provide a complete date of publication, including month and day, if it is on the early map. We must follow the rules in 2.16, under "Early

Printed Monographs" in Chapter 2 of AACR2R, and, more important, the sections in *Cartographic Materials,* under "Early cartographic items," for Place of publication (pp. 70-71), Publisher, distributor, etc. (pp. 75-76), and Date of publication (pp. 82-83).

Place of Publication

First, let us remember that place names do change with time, and, therefore, we may wish to provide the latest form of the name of a place of publication along with the form of the name found on the item. Rule 2.16B in AACR2R provides for just such a situation: "Transcribe the place of publication, etc., as it is found on the item. It may include the name(s) of publishers, printers, etc. Supply the modern name of the place if it is considered necessary for identification." The modern name, if supplied, should be in square brackets. The APPLICATION to Rule 4C8 in *Cartographic Materials* adds a couple of key points:

> Give the place of publication in the orthographic form and the grammatical case in which it appears in the source of information used. If the place of publication appears together with the name of a larger jurisdiction (e.g., country, state or similar designation), transcribe it as well.

The "orthographic form" mentioned here means in the form/spelling that is shown on the map as opposed to the form/spelling by which the place is known today.

The next item is not addressed in AACR2R at all, and this is one of the standout changes mentioned in the opening paragraph to this section. "Addresses" as we know them today, i.e., a number and street name specific to each home or business in the community, did not uniformly come into being until the twentieth century in this country, somewhat earlier in other countries. Historically, a business would hang a sign from the doorway with a picture and perhaps the name of the business upon it, and that served as an address for some time. Later, the sign and street name were often combined to form the local address of the business, in our case the printer. Therefore, the next rule in *Cartographic Materials,* Rule 4C9, specifies that "[i]f the full address or the sign of the publisher, etc., appears in the prescribed source of information, add it to the place if it aids in identifying or dating the item." The last part of this interpretation to Rule 2.16C in AACR2R regarding the sign of a publisher or printer quite often *does* assist, along with other indications, not only in dating an undated map but also in identifying different editions or "states" of early maps. In many instances, these maps may have had only minor changes applied to them, but changes in address or sign of the publisher/printer are telltale indicators that can be critical in historical cartography research or historical research of a particular place. Therefore, in most instances, it is helpful to add the sign and/or address of a publisher to the Place of publication area. A couple of examples from CM follow:

> Augsburg, in S. Katharinen Gassen
> London, Fleete Streate at the signe of the Blacke Elephant

What if *only* the address and/or sign of the publisher appears on the map? If this is the case, then Rule 4C10 in CM tells us to supply, in square brackets and in English, the actual place of publication and then record the address or sign within the publisher statement. Finally, make sure to include a note of justification for the English-language place of publication that you have supplied, if necessary.

If more than one place of publication is found on the item, "always record the first, and *optionally,* record the others in the order in which they appear." If you choose to ignore supplying the second or other places then add the abbreviation "etc." following the place of publication, in square brackets. This follows Rule 4C11 in CM. For example:

> Londres ; et se trouve `a Paris
> London [etc.]

Publisher, Printer, Etc.

Once again, practice for early maps differs from that with contemporary maps and other materials when it comes to providing the name of the publisher, printer, etc. Whereas for contemporary items, to provide a publisher's statement, the map must have a formal statement of publisher or an inferred publisher based on a copyright statement, using such terms as "issued," "made," "composed," "produced," "published," and others, a different set of terms describes the same function for historical maps. These terms include "bookseller," "bookseller-printer," or "printer," as outlined in Rule 4B9 in CM, and their meanings differ from those used for contemporary printers. Keep this difference in mind as you look for a publication statement on historical maps because these terms constitute a statement of publication as opposed to a separate statement of manufacturer.

In addition, we are allowed to shorten or abbreviate portions of a publisher's name for contemporary items, which differs from early maps. Rule 4D9 in CM instructs to "[r]ecord the rest of the details relating to the publisher, etc., as they are given in the item." The rest of this rule addresses a common occurrence with early maps, and that is the length of the publication statement as well as parts of the statement being separated physically on the map:

> Separate the parts of a complex publisher, etc., statement only if they are presented separately in the item. If the publisher, etc., statement includes the name of a printer, record it here. Omit words in the publisher, etc., statement that do not aid in the identification of the item and do not indicate the role of the publisher, etc. Indicate omissions by the mark of omission.

For example:

> London : Printed for the author and sold by J. Roberts
> Birmingham : Printed by John Baskerville for R. and J. Dodsley . . .
> London : Imprinted . . . by Robt. Barber . . . and by the assigns of John Bill

Once again, if there are two or more publisher's statements, we may provide both or all, but if we wish to provide only the first statement found on the item, then we must conclude the statement with the abbreviation "etc." in square brackets, as with multiple places of publication.

Date of Publication or Printing

Providing a date of publication, when it exists on an early map, is not too different from the practice with contemporary maps. However, some outstanding changes include the ability to provide a complete date of publication that includes month and/or day as well as year and sometimes having to take a long Latin date in a verbal form and convert it to an abbreviated numerical form. Also, remembering that we are dealing with items created at a time when other calendars may have been used and Roman numerals were more commonly used than today's Arabic numerals, we have to take some time to make conversions where necessary. Rule 4F10, and its *Optional* application, in CM addresses these situations:

> Give the date of publication or printing, including the day and month, as found in the item. Change roman numerals indicating the year to arabic numerals unless they are misprinted, in which case record the roman numeral and add a correction. Add the date in the modern chronology if this is considered to be necessary . . . [while the *Option* states] . . . formalize the date if the statement appearing in the item is very long.

Finally, as is the case with a contemporary map, Rule 4F11 in CM instructs us, "If the item is undated and the date of publication is unknown, give an approximate date." Naturally, place an approximate date in square brackets and add a question mark if it is warranted.

PHYSICAL DESCRIPTION CHANGES

The only notable differences in the physical description area for historical maps are the form of the map itself, manuscript in nature versus printed, and information specific to the media used for both drawing and coloring such maps. First, if the map is manuscript in form, indicate this using "ms." in the "Extent of item", or subfield "a", area of the 300 field according to Rule 3.5B1 in AACR2R. However, be aware that Library of Congress practice, as well as the practice denoted in *Cartographic Materials,* differs from the rules in that "ms." is placed in the "Other physical details" area, or subfield "b". For example:

- *AACR2R rules:*
  300   1 ms. map : |b col. ; |c 38 x 48 cm.
- *LC practice and interpretation in* Cartographic Materials:
  300   1 map : |b ms., col. ; |c 38 x 48 cm.

Therefore, you will likely notice both practices being applied in bibliographic records found on OCLC if you work with manuscript maps for any length of time. Finally, if the map being cataloged is in *manuscript* form, the designation "hand" is not needed because it is understood that the entire content of the manuscript map was created by hand, including the coloring method used.

In addition, if a printed map is hand colored, as was common practice for many years, this information was given in a note as opposed to being placed in the "Other physical details" area, according to AACR2R (1998 Edition). This practice was provided for in the rules in the notes area; specifically, see Rule 3.7B10 for notes on "Physical description" where you will find the term "Hand coloured" listed. Library of Congress practice differed from AACR2R, specifying that the method of coloring be placed in the "Other physical details" area by stating, "Include *hand col.* as 'other physical details' " (see "Hand Colored" on page 2.15 of the LC *Map Cataloging Manual*). In addition, the APPLICATION to Rule 5C3 in *Cartographic Materials* specifies, "If a printed item is hand colored, state this as 'hand col.' Do not differentiate between color and partial color."

However, a recently approved change in the rules allows the option of providing specifics regarding the medium used, including "hand col.", under new Rule 3.5C6 Medium, as part of "Other physical details". An example for a printed map would be:

300   1 map : |b hand col. in ink, mounted on linen ; |c 29 x 40 cm.

Note that in the order of "Other physical details" color comes before medium and material, thus the order of items in subfield "b" in the previous example.

NOTES UNIQUE TO AND NEEDED FOR HISTORICAL MAPS

As is the case for contemporary maps, notes that assist in completing a full description of the historical map are always warranted. Some notes used for contemporary maps take on added significance when used for historical maps, such as the "Covers . . ." note to assist the patron with understanding what part of the world's surface is shown on the map when names of places differed in the past or the title is misleading regarding the extent of the mapped area. For instance, "New Netherlands" had a clear meaning to people living in the seventeenth century but may be completely unknown today, and, therefore, a note describing which states in the United States "New Netherlands" once covered can be very helpful.

However, some unique notes come into play when working with these kinds of maps, as one would expect. Kandoian's (1999) article describes the purpose for each of the following notes that are unique to historical maps; therefore, a simple listing of these follows:

- *Dedication note:* Provide a quoted note for a dedication that appears on the map.
- *Statement of responsibility:* A couple of specific cases involve what are known as "precopyright" statements, one which usually begins "Entered according to an Act of Congress . . . [date]" and one called "Cum privilegio".
- *Source, edition, history notes:* Information discovered in the process of researching specific aspects of the source or edition of a particular map needs to be shared because it often distinguishes the map from similar ones. Notes of this type often begin with "From . . .", "Earlier ed. appears in . . .", and "Based on . . ."
- *Donor or previous owner notes*
- *Mathematical notes:* In particular, always specify the prime meridian used on the map and the map's orientation if it differs from north, which was often the case.
- *Physical description notes:* Most important is providing information about a watermark, as this is a unique physical marker that assists researchers in determining, with some accuracy, when the paper was printed and by whom.
- *Reference to published descriptions notes:* These assist other researchers in tracing the history of a particular title and/or further elucidating details regarding the map being cataloged.
- *Copy being described and copy specific notes:* The *copy being described* note should be placed in a 590 field and is introduced by a phrase that identifies the holding library, e.g., "Hargrett Rare Book and Manuscript Library copy imperfect . . .". The *copy specific* note is placed in the 500 field with a $5 and Library identifier and is used to describe further the physical char-

acteristics of the map not addressed in the 300 field, such as the aforementioned "hand colored" situation, when it is specific to the copy being described. Another typical note in this category involves references to particular annotations made on the map being cataloged.

SUBJECT SUBDIVISION PRACTICE TO EMPHASIZE THE HISTORICAL ASPECT

In most regards, subject access to historical maps and their content is the same as when working with contemporary maps. Subject headings for the geographic areas shown must be provided. Those maps which are topical in nature must receive appropriate topical subject headings as well as geographic subdivisions to specify where the topics are located. A major concern of historical maps, naturally, must be to bring out the historical aspect of the map, i.e., when in history was the map produced.

One large group of early maps is specified in terms of its history through the use of the subject subdivision "Early works to 1800", which always is the last part of the subject string. Unlike other chronological subdivisions, however, this particular subdivision is considered a genre term and therefore receives the subfield tag of "v", instead of "y". All maps produced before the year 1800 receive this subdivision, for example:

651 0   United States |v Maps |v Early works to 1800.

Maps produced from 1800 to 1900 do not necessarily need a chronological or historical subdivision, but in such cases the chronological subdivision of "19th century" may be used.

A difficult set of subdivisions that are often improperly used for historical maps includes "History" and "Historical geography". Because historical maps *are* documents of history themselves, as opposed to being *about* history, the subdivision of "History" is not necessary and is inaccurate. In one circumstance the subdivisions "History" or "Historical geography" can be appropriately applied. If the historical map records historic sites or events of an earlier time from that in which the map was produced, then one of these subdivisions may be used.

OTHER SUBJECT PRACTICES OF NOTE

As we move through time, activities of humans cause places to change names for a variety of reasons. One of the more common factors of name changes is war or other forms of conflict between nations or groups of individuals. And, naturally, as civilization moved through the Age of Discovery, when new lands were being discovered and subsequently named, later generations renamed specific cities, regions, and countries, again most usually through some form of conflict and conquest. The nature of place name changes can cause much consternation for the cataloger of historical maps. For instance, the map says "Cipangu" or "Chipangu" but we know this country today as Japan. Another example is the nation of "Siam," which eventually became what we know today as Thailand. A more modern equivalent of this type of name change was the renaming of Burma to Myanmar in 1990.

Fortunately, the good folk in the Geography and Map Division at the Library of Congress provided instruction on how to handle such name changes. The Library of Congress's *Subject Cataloging Manual,* in instruction H 708, specifies "to assign as a subject heading or as a geographic subdivision, only the latest name of a political jurisdiction that has had one or more earlier names, as long as the territorial identity remains essentially unchanged." Therefore, the map titled "Partie de l'Amerique septentrionale, qui comprend le cours de l'Ohio, la Nlle. Angleterre, la Nlle. York, le New Jersey, la Pensylvanie, le Maryland, la Virginie, la Caroline" (see Figure 18.1) would receive this subject heading:

651 0   United States – Maps – Early works to 1800.

because it shows what is part of the United States when our country was in its infancy. This map also received the subject heading "Ohio River Valley – Maps – Early works to 1800" because it is more specific to the present-day area covered by the map. Note in Figure 18.1 that the title states "l'Amerique septentrionale," which means "northern America," so it's important to note that this phrase could also include all or part of Canada, and in such cases a subject heading for Canada or even North America could be used, if warranted. The 500 "Covers . . ." note is critical to provide so that the user of the bibliographic record may gain firsthand knowledge of the geographic area

OCLC: 46606806   Rec stat: n

Entered: 20010327   Replaced: 20010327   Used: 20010327

Type: e   ELvl: I   Srce: d   Relf: i   Ctrl: Lang: fre

BLvl: m   Form: GPub: SpFm: MRec: Ctry: fr

CrTp: a   Indx: 0   Proj: DtSt: s   Dates: 1783,

Desc: a

```
 1  040     NYP |c NYP
 2  007     a |b j |d c |e a |f n |g z |h n
 3  034 1   a |b 2900000 |d W0900000 |e W0680000 |f N0460000 |g N0310000
 4  052     3700
 5  052     3707 |b O5
 6  090     |b
 7  049     UPMM
 8  100 1   Robert de Vaugondy, Gilles, |d 1688-1766.
```

9 245 10 Partie de l'Amerique septentrionale, qui comprend le cours de l'Ohio, la Nlle. Angleterre, la Nlle. York, le New Jersey, la Pensylvanie, le Maryland, la Virginie, la Caroline / |c par le Sr. Robert de Vaugondy, gâeographe ; Groux.

10 255   Scale [ca. 1:2,900,000] |c (W 90°--W 68°/N 46°--N 31°).

11 260   [Paris? : |b s.n., |c 1783?]

12 300   1 map : |b hand col. ; |c 47 x 63 cm.

13 500   Relief shown pictorially.

14 500   Covers the area from the Great Lakes to South Carolina and from the Atlantic coast to the Mississippi River.

15 500   Shows provinces, counties, towns and cities, rivers, Indian villages and tribal territory, and forts.

16 500   Later version of a map originally appearing in the author's Atlas universal. 1757 [i.e. 1758]

17 500   Prime meridian: Ferro.

18 500   "1783" handwritten in ink at base of cartouche. |5 NN

19 500   Watermark.

20 500   Includes inset, "Supplâement pour la Caroline."

21 510 4   Variant of LC Maps of North America, 1750-1789, |c 718

22 651 0   United States |v Maps |v Early works to 1800.

23 651 0   Ohio River Valley |v Maps |v Early works to 1800.

24 700 1   Groux.

FIGURE 18.1. Use of Present-Day Geographic Subject Headings for a Geographic Area Not Known by Its Current Name in the Time the Map Was Made (*Source:* WorldCat Database, the OCLC Online Union Catalog [WorldCat], see <http://www.oclc.org/firstsearch/database/details/dbinformation_WorldCat.html>.)

covered before he or she ever looks at the map itself, if the title of the map does not make this clear. Once again, base the choice of subject heading(s) on the geographic area covered as opposed to what the title says or implies.

Yet another frustrating situation faced when cataloging historical maps is the change of geographic area encompassed within one set of political boundaries, such as one large county within a state in the United States being split into two counties, or the growth and change of boundaries, such as how the United States itself came to be in its present form. In all such cases, the extent of the geographic area covered under present conditions is a determining factor of what geographic subject headings and subdivisions apply. Pay special attention to the matter of "as long as the territorial identity remains essentially unchanged" in H 708 of the *Subject Cataloging Manual* because this may determine whether the name of a former place is retained as a geographic subject heading.

An example of one such condition is provided by Kandoian (1999) in her article. It involves Queens County, New York. The map titled "New Map of Kings and Queens County, New York" by J. B. Beers and Company shows territory before 1899 that was at that time called Queens County but covers what is today Queens County and Nassau County. The subject headings for this situation are as follows:

651   0   Kings County (N.Y.) |v Maps.
651   0   Queens County (N.Y.) |v Maps.
651   0   Nassau County (N.Y.) |v Maps.

The cataloger then provides a note of justification describing the territorial situation as shown on the map for that time period. (If it is important to the particular local institution, free-form local headings for the historical name of the place can be added to the local bibliographic record.)

CONCLUSION

Working with historical maps is often very rewarding simply due to the more fanciful display of information, the age of the map itself, and the ability to witness a portion of our geographical past. However, due to the nature of how these maps were manufactured, produced, and distributed, as well as dealing with the known and unknown geography of the time, portions of the bibliographical description take on new twists. The earlier the map, the more often it can be attributed to a particular individual, quite the opposite of contemporary maps. And, although the physical description changes mostly with the provision of coordinates, the publication information and subject access do provide new opportunities for learning.

Chapter 19

Special Formats and Situations

Not all sheet maps are simply maps printed on pieces of paper to be stored in map case drawers; sometimes maps are mounted for specific purposes or created from a different original. "Classroom maps," which come on rollers that can be hung from a blackboard (or whiteboard these days) or wall or tripod-type of stand; facsimiles of historical maps; map series; etc., all present some additional or different descriptive work to be done. In addition, preservation practices may cause a need for additional information in the bibliographic record, at least at the local level, to assist the patron with either finding a map in a different location or alerting the individual to a change in circulation policy. These and other "special" situations are covered in this chapter, focusing particularly on changes and additions from ordinary contemporary monographic sheet maps that need to be highlighted in the record.

WALL MAPS, INCLUDING THOSE MOUNTED ON ROLLERS

Wall maps differ from "regular" sheet maps only in terms of their physical aspects. Therefore, subfield "b" in the Physical description area is used to provide details beyond simply the use of multiple colors on the map. In addition, because of their format, there is a need for an additional note or two, and the Special Format fixed field must be coded for "wall map" as a unique genre of maps.

Any physically large (or small for that matter) map can be hung on a wall, but large-sized maps *meant* to be mounted on a wall usually have hanging devices attached to them, either embedded in the map itself, as in the case of grommets, or attached to the back of the map, such as some kind of metal ring or cloth loop. Typically, older maps were also mounted on cloth or a stronger fiber surface to protect them from tearing by their own weight. Recent vintage wall maps are often printed on a paperlike plastic such as "Tyvec" or have been laminated to provide the necessary hanging strength. Wall maps should be coded "o" in the Special Format fixed field, given a note indicating what they are, e.g., "Wall map", and if a hanging device is part of the map, this should be included in the note, for example, "Wall map, includes metal grommets for hanging." Also, if the map was glued onto a cloth or other stronger backing this information is given in 300 subfield "b".

In the case of wall maps whose ends are mounted on rollers so that they can be hung in this manner, typically used in a classroom setting, the fact that they are mounted on wooden, plastic, or metal rollers can also be denoted in 300 subfield "b" (see Figure 19.1).

Optionally, LC practice has been not to give information about the rollers themselves in the Other physical details area with color and/or mounting information, but to include a note indicating that the item is a wall map and that it is mounted on rollers (see line 16 in Figure 19.2). Whichever method of description is used regarding the rollers themselves, i.e., the 300 subfield "b" or simply a note, code the Special Format fixed field as "o" and provide the necessary version of the "Wall map . . ." note. Sometimes these "rolled wall maps," as they are generically called, come with a metal tripod to hold them, and this information can be given in a note as well.

MAP SERIES AND COLLECTIONS—
SOME FURTHER COMMENTS AND SUGGESTIONS

Map series, and similarly "sets" or collections, those titles in which multiple physical single sheets are combined to provide geographic coverage of a moderate- to large-sized area, such as a country at a large scale, may be cataloged as a single title or each sheet in the group may be cataloged separately. Often map series or collections are also based on a particular topic, such as their being topographic in nature. Also, the series or collection may contain as few as eight or ten sheets or several hundred.

The decision to catalog a map series or collection as a single title versus as individual sheets must be made at the local level, although factors such as how many sheets the map collection holds in a given

OCLC: 47143841   Rec stat: n
Entered: 20010618   Replaced: 20010618   Used: 20010618
  Type: e   ELvl: I   Srce: d   Relf: d   Ctrl: Lang: eng
  BLvl: m   Form: GPub: SpFm: o   MRec: Ctry: enk
  CrTp: a   Indx: 0   Proj: DtSt: s   Dates: 1914,
  Desc: a

  1 040   UPM |c UPM
  2 007   a |b j |d c |e g |f n |g z |h n
  3 034 1   a |b 3220177 |d W0320000 |e E0720000 |f N0720000 |g N0280000
  4 043   e------
  5 052   5700
  6 052   5701
  7 052   6965
  8 052   7010
  9 090   G5700 1914 |b .E3
10 090 |b
11 049   UPMM
12 110 2 Edward Stanford Ltd.
13 245 10 Stanford's library map of Europe / |c Edward Stanford Ltd. ...
14 246 30 Library map of Europe
15 250   New ed. 1914.
16 255   Scale 1:3,220,177. 50.8235 miles = 1 in. |c (W 32°--E 72°/N 72°--N 28°).
17 260   London : |b Edward Stanford, Ltd., |c 1914.
18 300   1 map : |b col., mounted on cloth and rollers ; |c 142 x 157 cm.
19 500   Also shows Russia, Turkey, "Asia Minor", and a small portion of northern Africa.
20 500   Relief shown by hachures.
21 500   Wall map.
22 500   In lower right margin: Stanford's Geographical Establishment, London.
23 500   In lower left margin: Stanford's library series.
24 500   "London: Published ... September 7th, 1914."
25 500   Includes bar "Scales of national measures."
26 651 0 Europe |v Maps.
27 651 0 Europe |x History |y 1871-1918 |v Maps.
28 651 0 Europe, Eastern |v Maps.

FIGURE 19.1. Indication of a Wall Map on Rollers Using the 300 Subfield "b" Area (*Source:* WorldCat Database, the OCLC Online Union Catalog [WorldCat], see <http://www.oclc.org/firstsearch/database/details/dbinformation_WorldCat.html>.)

OCLC: 40424616   Rec stat: c

Entered: 19981110   Replaced: 20010630   Used: 19990807

 Type: e   ELvl: Srce: Relf: g   Ctrl: Lang: eng

 BLvl: m   Form: GPub: SpFm: o   MRec: Ctry: flu

 CrTp: a   Indx: 1   Proj: ca   DtSt: s   Dates: 1998,

 Desc: a

 1 010   98-680908

 2 040   DLC |c DLC |d OCL

 3 007   a |b j |d c |e a |f n |g z |h n

 4 034 1   a |b 2500000 |d W1280000 |e W0660000 |f N0500000 |g N0230000

 5 050 00 G3700 1998 |b .C8

 6 052   3700

 7 090 |b

 8 049   UPMM

 9 110 2 Custom Cartographics (Firm)

10 245 10 United States / |c cartography by Custom Cartographics.

11 255   Scale [ca. 1:2,500,000] ; |b Albers equal-area proj. |c (W 128°--W
66°/N 50°--N 23°).

12 260   Lake Monroe, FL : |b UniversalMAP, |c c1998.

13 300   1 map : |b col. ; |c 126 x 191 cm.

14 500   Relief shown by spot heights.

15 500   Also shows time zones.

16 500   Wall map mounted on wooden rods for hanging.

17 500   Accompanied by: United States wall map, index to cities and towns.
19 p. ; 28 cm.

18 500   Insets: Alaska -- Hawaii -- Puerto Rico, Virgin Islands.

19 651 0 United States |v Maps.

20 650 0 Time |x Systems and standards |z United States |v Maps.

21 710 2 Universal Map (Firm)

FIGURE 19.2. Library of Congress Practice for Showing a Wall Map Mounted on Rollers Using a 500 Note (*Source:* WorldCat Database, the OCLC Online Union Catalog [WorldCat], see <http://www.oclc.org/firstsearch/database/details/ dbinformation_WorldCat.html>.)

title, the relative importance of providing sheet-level itemization, and simply the number of individuals doing the cataloging work will influence the outcome. However, if the decision is to catalog a map collection or map series as a single title, then the cataloger must be aware of some subtle differences in the description and in the coding of a couple of fields as well.

First, in describing a map series/collection, the mental aspect to maintain is always remember that one is cataloging the title as a group and, therefore, no one sheet in that group takes precedence over any of the others. In fact, if one or two sheets or a minimal number in a very large map group differ slightly in some manner, such as in the wording of the title, these should be considered exceptions and either additional notes or title entries can be used to highlight the differences. Consider "majority rules" or even the tried-and-true "80/20" rule of thumb for each descriptive part of the record. For example, if the majority of sheets in the series/collection indicate that they were produced using the Transverse Mercator projection, while a minority were created using a different projection, then the Projection fixed field should be coded "bh" and the 255 subfield "b" should contain "Transverse Mercator proj." A note can then be given to indicate the number of sheets where the differing projection comes into play. Following are the parts of the bibliographic record that need to be coded or described differently for map series/collections.

- "Cartographic Type" or "CrTp" *fixed field:* Code this as "b".

- *090 local LC-type call number:* Replace the date of situation with a designation for the scale of the series or collection; if all sheets are at the same scale, give this in the abbreviated form, e.g., "s50" for 1:50,000 (see page 1.18 in the LC *Map Cataloging Manual* for specifics on a range of scales and how the abbreviated form is created and Chapter 15, "Scale statement in the call number for map series or collections"). If the sheets involve two or more different scales, then use the abbreviation "svar", meaning "scales vary." Do *not* confuse this with the use of "Scale varies" or "Scales differ" in the 255 field; in fact, this situation is more accurately of the "scales differ" type.

- *Title:* Provide/use a collective title for map series or collections; individual sheet titles do not count unless used as a "Part title" after the collective title when cataloging the individual sheets as separate monographs, in which case it would be placed in subfield "p" in the 245 field. Often map collections and map series titles include geographic area and scale or vice versa, e.g., British Guiana 1:50,000, or 1:50,000 British Guiana, depending on the layout and typography (see Figure 19.3). If a collective title is not available then create one that includes the geographic area and the scale if it is a single scale. Naturally, enclose a provided title in square brackets and give the "Title supplied by cataloger" note. Finally, and this is optional, the cataloger

OCLC: 47624958   Rec stat: n

Entered: 20010721   Replaced: 20010721   Used: 20010721

 Type: e   ELvl: I   Srce: d   Relf: dg   Ctrl: Lang: eng

 BLvl: m   Form: GPub: f   SpFm: MRec: Ctry: enk

 CrTp: b   Indx: 0   Proj: bd   DtSt: s   Dates: 1959,

 Desc: a

 1 040   UPM |c UPM

 2 007   a |b j |d a |e a |f n |g z |h n

 3 034 1   a |b 50000 |d W0610000 |e W0563000 |f N0090000 |g N0010000

 4 043   s-gy---

 5 052   5250

 6 090   G5250 s50 |b .G73

 7 090 |b

 8 049   UPMM

 9 110 1   Great Britain. |b Directorate of Overseas Surveys.

 10 245 10 British Guiana 1:50,000 |h [map] / |c third edition revised by D.O.S. 1958 from 1:25,000 maps and other data prepared by Lands and Mines Dept., 1954.

 11 250   3rd ed.

 12 255   Scale 1:50,000 ; |b transverse Mercator proj., meridian of origin 59° west of Greenwich, latitude of origin, equator |c (W 61°00'--W 56°30'/N 9°00'--N 1°00').

 13 260   [Tolworth, Surrey?] : |b Published by Directorate of Overseas Surveys, |c 1959.

 14 300   maps ; |c 56 x 56 cm., on sheets 84 x 64 cm.

 15 490 1   D.O.S. ; |v 40 (Series E791)

 16 500   Relief shown by hachures and spot heights.

 17 500   Also shows the location of aerial flight path by reel number.

 18 500   Standard map series designation: Series E791.

 19 500   "Field Survey Data supplied by Lands and Mines Dept. and D.O.S. Air photography by Air Survey Co. Ltd., Sept. 1950."

 20 500   Sheets individually numbered.

 21 500   Includes adjoining sheets index and notes.

 22 500   "1250/8/59 O.S."--the month changes for each sheet in the set.

 23 651 0 Guyana |v Maps.

 24 710 1   British Guiana. |b Dept. of Lands and Mines.

 25 710 2   Air Survey Co. Ltd.

 26 740 01 Series E791.

FIGURE 19.3. Example of Map Series with Collective Title (*Source:* WorldCat Database, the OCLC Online Union Catalog [WorldCat], see <http://www.oclc.org/firstsearch/database/details/dbinformation_WorldCat.html>.)

may give the individual sheet titles in a Contents note if he or she thinks it is important to provide this level of information for the patron.

• *Variant titles:* Use the 246 field to bring out a variant of the title given in the 245, such as the case noted previously for British Guiana. If typography indicates that "British Guiana" should come first in the title then include the alternate form of the title where the scale comes first in this field. The other title that might be included here is the one or two titles in the series or collection where the wording differs slightly but may have an impact on retrieval. Using the British Guiana example again, some of the sheets may have the later form of the name and, thus, "British Guyana 1:50,000" may need to be given.

• *Edition:* Many factors may influence whether the entire map series/collection is of a single edition; i.e., all of the sheets were published at the same time under a numbered or named edition, or individual sheets have different edition statements. Perhaps a country focuses on reissuing some sheets in a series more quickly than others because they cover an urban area where change is more rapid. Or, during the history of the creation of the map series, a country's national mapping agency changed and therefore some portions of the country were re-mapped and issued as a later edition while other portions were never updated. Make an effort to check edition statements on all or most of the sheets; if a single edition statement is on all of them use it, and if two or more editions are noted then use the statement "Various ed."

• *Scale:* Note the discussion in Chapter 11, "Mathematical Data Area" on maps with two or more scales. If the series/collection is all at the same scale, then treat the scale statement as you would for a single map. If the maps involved are at two different scales, then give both, and if they are at three or more scales, then give "Scales differ".

• *Publication date(s):* Due to the nature of map series and collections, it often takes more than one year for a title to be completed. While this is not always the case, do expect to give a range of publication dates for a completed series/collection or to provide an open date for a title that is not complete.

• *Physical description area:* This is where some major differences appear in the record as opposed to when cataloging single maps, and it is also where one can quickly determine that a bibliographic record is for a map series/collection as opposed to a single map. The tip-off is in the Extent of item area of the 300 field; for map series and collections the number of maps is *not* given; instead the word "maps" is provided alone. Then, in the Dimensions area, the size of the maps is given; if they are all of the same size (remember to measure between the neat lines!), then give the statement "each 55 x 46 cm."; if they are of two different sizes, then give both of them; if they are of three or more sizes, then give the largest top-to-bottom dimension of all of the maps and the largest side-to-side dimension of all of the maps followed by "or smaller". Also in the Dimensions area, the number of *sheets* can be given if the counting is relatively easy. The same methodology is employed in giving the sheet sizes, and the sheet size should always be given for map series and collections. For example:

> 300   maps : |b col. ; |c each 55 x 46 cm., on sheets
> 65 x 50 cm.
> 300   maps : |b col. ; |c 55 x 46 cm. and 50 x 46 cm., on sheets
> 65 x 50 cm.
> 300   maps : |b col. ; |c 84 x 59 cm. or smaller, on sheets
> 90 x 62 cm.
> 300   maps : |b col. ; |c 84 x 59 cm. or smaller, on sheets
> 90 x 62 cm. and 86 x 60 cm.
> 300   maps : |b col. ; |c 84 x 59 cm. or smaller, on sheets
> 95 x 65 cm. or smaller.

What happens if not all of the sheets are in color or if all of the sheets are in a single color? The latter case is obvious: the subfield "b" is not used at all (unless mounting comes into play). However, when some of the maps are in multiple colors and some are not, then, depending on the ease of counting, either give the number of sheets that are in color or not in color or use the phrase "some" or "most" as part of the statement. For example:

> 300   maps : |b col., 2 b and w ; |c . . .
> 300   maps : |b col. (some b & w) : |c . . .
> 300   maps : |b 5 col. ; |c . . .
> 300   maps : |b some col. ; |c

• *Notes:* As mentioned earlier, employ additional notes to bring out "exceptions" within the series/collection. Also, if this can be easily determined either by a hand count or because a sheet index was given on the maps, try always to give a "Geographic coverage complete in *x* sheets" note.

To summarize, treat a map series or collection as a group and describe it as such in the bibliographic record. This means using a collective title, i.e., a title that appears on each map and by which the entire group of maps is known; changing the Physical description area to fit the situation of describing multiple maps as opposed to a single map; encoding the Cartographic Type fixed field correctly and the other fixed fields for the series/collection as a whole when two or more individual sheets differ; and making sure to use the scale in the call number as opposed to a date of situation.

TEXTS, INDEXES, AND OTHER SUPPLEMENTARY ITEMS

Over the years I've been asked about how to handle supplementary items that come with a map, such as an accompanying text or a separate legend sheet. Chapter 9 in *Cartographic Materials* explains what to do in such cases extremely well, covering how to describe supplementary items that are independent (catalog them separately and provide a reference to the map in the note area) and those items which are dependent with the map. Let's look at texts, indexes, legend sheets, and such that are linked to maps and therefore "dependent" upon them. Naturally, this is a discussion about items issued with the map, not those items which are later separated by the map librarian or map cataloger at the local level for reasons such as storing them flat.

Rule 9B in *Cartographic Materials* provides for three methods by which to handle dependent supplementary items; use subfield "e" in the Physical description area, provide a note describing the item and linking it to the map, and use a multilevel description. In the first two cases, a good rule of thumb for choosing to use 300 subfield "e" versus a note is whether the title of the supplementary item is identical to or nearly matches the title of the map. If it nearly matches or does match the title of the map, then providing the extent and physical description in the 300 field using subfield "e" may be enough. For example, many geologic maps include accompanying explanatory text in which the title varies only with the use of a linking phrase, such as "Explanatory notes to . . ." or ". . . notice explicative." In such a case, add to the Physical Description field the accompanying material subfield, i.e., subfield "e", for example:

> 300   1 map : |b col. ; |c 48 x 36 cm. + |e text (12 p. : tables, ill. ; 28 cm.)

Also, generally, if the accompanying item is a single sheet with a legend on it or a separate index or gazetteer, these are usually shown by using subfield "e"; identifying the specific item as "1 legend", "1 index", "legend sheet", "index sheet", or "gazetteer" followed by the dimensions of the sheet.

However, if the title of the text and the title of the map are completely different, then it is more helpful to the patron to provide the title of the text, along with its author, publication information, and physical description in an "Accompanies" or "Accompanied by" note. For example:

> 300   1 map : |b col. ; |c 48 x 36 cm.
> 500   Accompanied by: The stratigraphy and geology of the Sinking Creek quadrangle / by John P. Smith. Denver : Geological Survey of Colorado, 1998. (12 p. : tables, ill. ; 23 cm.).

In addition, *at the local level,* it may be important to provide the call number of the accompanying item if it will be shelved in a location separate from the map itself so that the patron, or the reference staff assisting the patron, can easily retrieve both items since they were intended to be used jointly.

FACSIMILES, PHOTOCOPIES, AND ASSORTED REPRODUCTIONS

The best source of information about how to handle facsimiles, photocopies, and other reproductions are both *Cartographic Materials,* pages 155-156, and the LC *Map Cataloging Manual,* Chapter 8. Each describes in detail how to handle the description of these items, although the LC *Map Cataloging Manual* is much more detailed and also assists with the classification of reprints. The bottom line for these kinds of materials is that one describes the facsimile, photocopy, or reproduction/reprint itself and provides details regarding the original, if available, in the Original Version, or 534, note. Rule 11A in *Cartographic Materials* explicitly states

> In describing a facsimile, photocopy, or other reproduction of atlases, maps, manuscripts, and graphic items, give all the data relating to the facsimile, etc., in the all areas except the note area. Give data relating to the original in the note area.

For more specific details, see either of the sources given earlier, and to determine how to create a 534 note, use OCLC's *Bibliographic Formats and Standards* in conjunction with the LC *Map Cataloging Manual*.

Appendix

Basic Maps Tagging Exercises

"PROJ:" FIXED FIELD AND 034
MATHEMATICAL DATA CODES

Supply the appropriate fixed field code for the Projection fixed field when appropriate and fill in the indicator value and correct information, including subfield tags, for the 034 field to match the 255 field.

1. 255   Scale [ca. 1:32,000].
    Proj: ___ 034 _ _____
2. 255   Scale [ca. 1:7,500]. Not "1 in. = 200 ft."
    Proj: ___ 034 _ _____
3. 255   Scale not given.
    Proj: ___ 034 _ _____
4. 255   Scale ca. 1:35,000,000 $c (W 150°--W 170°/N 80°--
            S 60°).
    Proj: ___ 034 _ _____
5. 255   Scale [ca. 1:28,500] ; $b Polyconic proj.
    Proj: ___ 034 _ _____
6. 255   Scale varies.
    Proj: ___ 034 _ _____
7. 255   Scale 1:14,000--1:32,000 ; $b Fuller proj.
    Proj: ___ 034 _ _____
8. 255   Scales differ.
    Proj: ___ 034 _ _____
9. 255   Scale 1:14,000,000. 1 in. = 221 statute miles at the
            Equator ; $b Mercator proj. $c (W 180°--E 180°/
            N 84°--S 70°).
    Proj: ___ 034 _ _____
10. 255   Not drawn to scale.
    Proj: ___ 034 _ _____

052 FIELD (GEOGRAPHIC AREA CODE)

Supply the appropriate class code based on the following call numbers and subject headings.

1. 050 0   G3312.S9P57 1981 |b .A3
    Shipwrecks -- Superior, Lake -- Maps.
    052   _____

2. 050 0   G3200 1981 |b .U5
    World maps.
    052   _____

3. 050 0   G3201.K1 1981 |b .F6
    Wood as fuel -- Maps.
    World maps.
    052   _____

4. 050 0   G4874.B3 s04 |b .C3
    Balboa (Panama) -- Maps, Tourist.
    052   _____

5. 050 0   G4201.P2 year |b .A5
    Roads -- Kansas -- Maps.
    Roads -- Nebraska -- Maps.
    052   _____
    052   _____

6. 050 0   G4154.C6 1981 |b .G3
    Clinton (Iowa) -- Maps.
    Camanche (Iowa) -- Maps.
    052   _____

7. 050 0   G3762.B6A35 1890 |b .B52
    Boston Bay (Mass.) -- Aerial views.
    Boston Region (Mass.) -- Aerial views.
    052   _____
    052   _____

8. 050 0   G3201.P55 1981 |b .I6
    Ships -- Maintenance and repair -- Maps.
    World maps.
    052   _____

300 FIELD (PHYSICAL DESCRIPTION)

Create a complete 300 field, including correct subfield codes and punctuation, for the following descriptions of cartographic items.

1. A colored map 75 cm. high x 16 cm. wide.

2. 3 colored maps on 3 sheets of paper; the maps range in size from 25 cm. to 40 cm. high and from 59 to 79 cm. wide; the sheets of paper are all 52 cm. high and 100 cm. wide.

3. 3 colored maps on 1 sheet of paper; each map is 10 cm. high by 20 cm. wide; 2 maps are on 1 side of the sheet; the third is on the other side; the sheet is 46 cm. wide by 23 cm. high, folded to 22 x 28 cm., in an envelope 23 x 28 cm.

4. An atlas with colored maps and colored photographs, 45 cm. high x 25 cm. wide.

5. A map, printed in brown ink, 22 cm. high x 49 cm. wide.

6. A manuscript map on silk, hand colored, 22 cm. high x 49 cm. wide.

7. A map titled "Georgia : a geographic portrait" that contains six maps that are all on the same side of the sheet, each 10 x 13 cm., on a sheet 50 x 90 cm.; the maps are all colored.

8. A United States Forest Service map, colored, on a sheet 49 x 95 cm.; the map continues from one side to the other.

9. A National Geographic Society map, colored, bled to the edges (i.e., no neat line), on a sheet 39 x 53 cm.

10. A geological map of Bolivia, colored, 49 x 103 cm. accompanied by a pamphlet, "Mapa geologico de Bolivia, nota explicative", by Juan Cortez, published in 1980; it is 52 pages in length and is 23 cm. high x 14 cm. wide.

ANSWER SHEET

"Proj:" Fixed Field and 034 Mathematical Data Codes

1. Proj: ___ 034 <u>1</u> a |b 32000
2. Proj: ___ 034 <u>1</u> a |b 7500
3. Proj: ___ 034 <u>0</u> a
4. Proj: ___ 034 <u>1</u> a |b 35000000 |d W1500000 |e W1700000
   |f N0800000 |g S0600000
5. Proj: <u>cp</u>   034 <u>1</u> a |b 28500
6. Proj: ___ 034 <u>0</u> a
7. Proj: <u>zz</u>   034 <u>3</u> a |b 14000 |b32000
8. Proj: ___ 034 <u>0</u> a
9. Proj: <u>bd</u>   034 <u>1</u> a |b 14000000 |d W1800000 |e E1800000
   |f N0840000 |g S0700000
10. Proj: ___ 034 <u>0</u> a

052 Field (Geographic Area Code)

1. 052   <u>3312 |b S9</u>
2. 052   <u>3200</u>
3. 052   <u>3201</u>
4. 052   <u>4874 |b B3</u>
5. 052   <u>4201</u>
   052   <u>4191</u>
6. 052   <u>4154 |b C6 |b C15</u>
7. 052   <u>3762 |b B6</u>
   052   <u>3764 |b B6</u>
8. 052   <u>3201</u>

300 Field (Physical Description)

1. 1 map : $b col. ; $c 75 x 16 cm.
2. 3 maps : $b col. ; $c 40 x 79 cm. or smaller, sheets 52 x 100 cm.
3. 3 maps on 1 sheet : $b both sides, col. ; $c each 10 x 20 cm., sheet 23 x 46 cm., folded in envelope 23 x 28 cm.
4. $b col. ill., col. maps ; $c 45 cm.
5. 1 map ; $c 22 x 49 cm.
6. 1 ms. map : $b col., silk ; $c 22 x 49 cm. [add a 500 note "Hand colored."]
7. 6 maps on 1 sheet : $b col. ; $c each 10 x 13 cm., sheet 50 x 90 cm.
8. 1 map : $b both sides, col. ; $c on sheet 49 x 95 cm.

9. 1 map : $b col. ; $c 39 x 53 cm.
10. 1 map : $b col. ; $c 49 x 103 cm. + $e text (with a note as shown below)
    Or
    1 map : $b col. ; $c 49 x 103 cm. + $e text (52 p. ; 23 cm.)
    Note: Accompanied by: Mapa geologico de Bolivia, nota explicative /
    Juan Cortez. 1980. (52 p. ; 23 cm.).

Bibliography

Andrew, Paige G. and Lucinda M. Hall (1999). Teaching the Basics of Map Cataloging, *Catholic Library World* 69(4): 12-19.

Andrew, Paige G. and Mary Lynette Larsgaard (1999). *Maps and Related Cartographic Materials: Cataloging, Classification, and Bibliographic Control.* Binghamton, NY: The Haworth Information Press.

Anglo-American Cataloguing Committee for Cartographic Materials (AACCCM) (1982). *Cartographic Materials: A Manual of Interpretation for AACR2.* Chicago: American Library Association.

Anglo-American Cataloguing Rules, Second Edition, 1998 Revision (1999). Chicago: American Library Association.

Armstrong, HelenJane and Jimmie Lundgren (1999). "Cataloging Aerial Photographs and Other Remote-Sensing Materials." In Andrew, Paige G. and Mary Lynette Larsgaard (Eds.), *Maps and Related Cartographic Materials: Cataloging, Classification, and Bibliographic Control.* Binghamton, NY: The Haworth Information Press, pp. 165-227.

Boggs, Samuel Whittemore and Dorothy Cromwell Lewis (1963). *The Classification and Cataloging of Maps and Atlases.* New York: Special Libraries Association.

Chan, Lois Mai (1995). *Library of Congress Subject Headings: Principles and Applications,* Third Edition. Englewood, CO: Libraries Unlimited, Inc.

_____ (1999). *A Guide to the Library of Congress Classification,* Fifth Edition. Englewood, CO: Libraries Unlimited, Inc.

Drazniowsky, Roman (1975). *Map Librarianship: Readings.* Metuchen, NJ: Scarecrow Press.

Foreign Maps (1970). Washington, DC: U.S. Department of the Army (Technical Manual; TM 5-248).

Free-Floating Subdivisions: An Alphabetical Index, Twelfth Edition (2000). Prepared by the Cataloging Policy and Support Office. Washington, DC: Library of Congress, Cataloging Distribution Service.

Hughes, Glenda Jo Fox and Constance Demetracopoulos (Eds.), assisted by Mary H. Galneder (1997). *Map Cataloging Bibliography: Selectively Annotated* (Special Publication, Geography and Map Division, Special Libraries Association, No. 4). Washington, DC: Special Libraries Association.

Kandoian, Nancy A. (1999). "Cataloging Early Printed Maps." In Andrew, Paige G. and Mary Lynette Larsgaard (Eds.), *Maps and Related Cartographic Materials:*

Cataloging, Classification, and Bibliographic Control. Binghamton, NY: The Haworth Information Press, pp. 229-264.

Larsgaard, Mary Lynette (1978). *Map Librarianship: An Introduction.* Littleton, CO: Libraries Unlimited, Inc.

_____ (1998). "Classification" and "Cataloging." In *Map Librarianship: An Introduction.* Third Edition. Littleton, CO: Libraries Unlimited, pp. 117-155, 157-203.

LC Period Subdivisions Under Names of Places, Fifth Edition (1994). Compiled by the Office for Subject Cataloging Policy. Washington, DC: Library of Congress, Cataloging Distribution Service.

Library of Congress Subject Headings, Twenty-Fifth Edition (2002). Prepared by the Cataloging Policy and Support Office, Library of Congress. Washington, DC: Library of Congress, Cataloging Policy and Support Office.

Map Cataloging Manual (1991). Prepared by Geography and Map Division, Library of Congress. Washington, DC: Cataloging Distribution Service, Library of Congress.

Merriam-Webster's Geographical Dictionary, Third Edition (1998). Springfield, MA: Merriam-Webster, Inc.

Moore, Susan (1999). "Navigating the G Schedule." In Andrew, Paige G. and Mary Lynette Larsgaard (Eds.), *Maps and Related Cartographic Materials: Cataloging, Classification, and Bibliographic Control.* Binghamton, NY: The Haworth Information Press, pp. 375-384.

Parker, Velma (1999). "Cataloguing Map Series and Serials." In Andrew, Paige G. and Mary Lynette Larsgaard (Eds.), *Maps and Related Cartographic Materials: Cataloging, Classification, and Bibliographic Control.* Binghamton, NY: The Haworth Information Press, pp. 65-101.

Rand McNally Commercial Atlas and Marketing Guide (Annual). Chicago, IL: Rand McNally & Co.

Robinson, Arthur, Randall Sale, and Joel Morrison (1978). *Elements of Cartography,* Fourth Edition. New York: John Wiley & Sons.

Rockwell, Ken (1999). "Problem Areas in the Descriptive Cataloging of Sheet Maps." In Andrew, Paige G. and Mary Lynette Larsgaard (Eds.), *Maps and Related Cartographic Materials: Cataloging, Classification, and Bibliographic Control.* Binghamton, NY: The Haworth Information Press, pp. 39-63.

Salinger, Florence A. and Eileen Zagon (1984). *Notes for Catalogers: A Sourcebook for Use with AACR2.* White Plains, NY: Knowledge Industry Publications, Inc.

Saye, Jerry D. and Sherry L. Velluci (1989). *Notes in the Catalog Record: Based on AACR2 and LC Rule Interpretations.* Chicago: American Library Association.

Subject Cataloging Manual: Shelflisting, Second Edition (1995). Prepared by the Cataloging and Support Office, Library of Congress. Washington, DC: Library of Congress, Cataloging and Support Office.

Subject Cataloging Manual: Subject Headings, Fifth Edition, with updates through 2000 interfiled (2000). Prepared by the Office of Subject Cataloging Policy, Library of Congress. Washington, DC: Library of Congress, Cataloging Distribution Service.

Weimer, Kathryn H. (1999). "Subject Analysis for Cartographic Materials." In Andrew, Paige G. and Mary Lynette Larsgaard (Eds.), *Maps and Related Cartographic Materials: Cataloging, Classification, and Bibliographic Control.* Binghamton, NY: The Haworth Information Press, pp. 385-404.

Wynar, Bohdan S., with the assistance of Arlene Taylor Dowell and Jeanne Osborn (1980). "Description of Cartographic Materials." In *Introduction to Cataloging and Classification,* Sixth Edition. Littleton, CO: Libraries Unlimited, pp. 108-123.

Index

AAA, 12, 62, 188
AACR2R. *See Anglo-American Cataloguing Rules (AACR2R)*
Added entries, 150-151
  circumstances warranting, 185
  corporate bodies, 186-187
  justification for, 188-189
  personal names, 186
  potential, 188
  titles, 187
  tracing for cartographic publishers, 187-188
Additional information notes, 149-150
Alexandria Digital Initiative (ADI), 42
American Automobile Association (AAA), 12, 62, 188
Ancillary maps, 12, 13
Andrew, Paige G., 6-7, 121
Anglo-American Cataloguing Rules (AACR2R), 19
  coordinates, 95, 97
  physical description, 131, 135, 144, 203-204
  prominence, 61
  publication information, 109, 114, 200
  scale statement, 85, 86
  title, 194-195
Armitage, Geoff, 197
Armstrong, HelenJane, 121
Arrow Map Company, 188
Atlas, G classification for, 159

Bar scale, 80
Bar Scale Values table, 25
Bibliographic Formats and Standards (OCLC), 21, 34, 221
Bleeding edge, 140-141
Bounding coordinates, 94-96, 101-104

Bulletin (Special Libraries Association Geography and Map Division), 164

Cartographic Materials: A Manual of Interpretation for AACR2 (AACCCM), 12, 20
  added entries, 150-151
  coordinates, 95, 97, 99
  equivalencies for historical measurements, 196-197
  physical description, 131-132, 135, 144, 203-204
  publication information, 113-114, 200-201
  reproductions, 220-221
  scale statement, 85, 86
  scattered title phenomenon, 68-71
  statement of responsibility, 60, 61
  supplementary items, 219-220
  terminology, 118, 119
  title, 66, 194-195
  transferring from historic to Greenwich prime meridian, 199
Cartographic specific material designations (SMDs), 121-122
Cataloger's Desktop (software), 22, 172
"Cataloging Aerial Photographs and Other Remote-Sensing Materials" (Armstrong and Lundgren), 121
Cataloging and Classification Quarterly, 22, 169
Cataloging calculator, 25
"Cataloging Early Printed Maps" (Kandoian), 193
"Cataloging Map Series and Serials" (Parker), 118

233